The Greenhouse Church

Craig Taylor

Parson's Porch Books

The Greenhouse Church
ISBN: Softcover 978-1-951472-77-1
Copyright © 2020 by Craig Taylor

All rights reserved. No part of this book may be reproduced or transmitted in any form or by any means, electronic or mechanical, including photocopying, recording, or by any information storage and retrieval system, without permission in writing from the publisher.

The Greenhouse Church

Dedicated to my wife,

Tamara Susan Taylor,

who invests in the development of others.

Contents

Introduction 9
    Time to Grow!

Chapter One 14
    Start with Story

Chapter Two 27
    Understanding Your Role

Chapter Three 68
    Current Temperature

Chapter Four 91
    Gardening Tips

Chapter Five 105
    Time to Go!

Postscript 117
    Reflection Upon the Study

Appendix A 119
    E-MAIL Interview of Pastors (EIP)

Appendix B 122
    Leadership Development Audit (LDA)

Appendix C 127
    Revised LDA For Pastors In Sample

Appendix D 130
    Additional Follow-up Questions for Lay Leaders

Appendix E 131
    Questions for Discovering Life Purpose

Appendix F 134
    Questions to Consider in the Model for Leadership Development

Bibliography 137

Introduction
Time to Grow!

GREENHOUSES have a rich history. They have a noble beginning as well. According to Pliny the Elder, when royal physicians informed the emperor Tiberius in first century Rome that he should eat a cucumber a day, construction began on a special house for plants. The material for the roof allowed sunlight to enter and the walls of stone permitted heat from fires outside to warm the air inside. This early greenhouse assured a continual supply of cucumbers, which in turn preserved the health of the ruler of the Roman Empire.

Since the first century, greenhouses have continued to evolve. Materials such as glass, fiberglass, and plastic have replaced the stone walls and early roof made from mica or selenite. Contemporary heating systems, fans, and computers are now available to maintain the correct air temperature for a plethora of crops. The physical materials, construction methods, and techniques have changed over the years; however, the purpose has remained the same.

We still need greenhouses to ensure a continual supply of certain crops. With the aid of a greenhouse, a gardener can determine the temperature and humidity that the plants need. The greenhouse offers a place of protection. Although careful maintenance is still required, a greenhouse aids in the development of desired outcomes.

The local church has significant correlations to a greenhouse. The local church was born to be a place where God's people grow. The King of Kings ushered in the church to not only protect his children from false teachers, but also to feed his sheep. Over the years, the physical shape of the church building has changed. Bricks, mortar, and steel have replaced the open fields and tents where people used to gather to hear the Word. Contemporary sound and lighting systems have replaced the simple amenities of house churches. The purpose of the local church, however, remains unchanged. The local church is still the place where God's people grow to become spiritual leaders.

Some pastors and church leaders have drifted away from the church's purpose. The church is not a club or a business, although some attitudes and behaviors that prevail in some churches would indicate otherwise. In order to provide optimal spiritual growth among believers and produce spiritual leaders, the church must recover its purpose. The local church must return to what it was intended to be—a greenhouse. That is what my church experience over the years has taught me.

Although I desire to become who God intended for me to be, I have found it difficult to focus on my areas of strength instead of constantly worrying about meeting people's expectations of me. I felt confined for the first ten years of my professional pastoral ministry. After serving in four churches for an average of 2 ½ years in each church, I pleaded with God for anything different than another assignment that robbed me from me. I was an emerging leader hungry for opportunities to learn and grow. My passion was to help others discover their God-given strengths and give ministry away. However, most of my time was spent attending meetings, planning youth activities, leading Bible studies, and putting out fires. I wish things were different in the local church.

During my second church assignment, I began to read books on leadership. After the church board in my third church asked me to resign, I read everything I could get my hands-on concerning leadership in the church. I was asked to resign because I was the second pastor of a forty-year-old-church. The founding pastor had no ministerial education and led the church for thirty-seven years. Everything I tried to do was met with skepticism. Finally, an individual was elected to the church board who successfully rallied the other church board members around him. I showed up to the monthly board meeting and received a request for my resignation. After consulting with my district superintendent, I gave them what they wanted. When I interviewed 2 ½ years earlier, the elected leaders in this church said that they wanted a pastor who could teach them how to minister to their community. Later I realized that they wanted different results than they had experienced in the past without making any changes to what they were used to doing. After that experience was when my interest in leadership literature really began. I desired to find a better way to lead the church to become all that God intended the church to be.

After searching for another pastoral assignment for six months, my fourth full-time ministry experience since graduating from seminary was much like the other three. I was asked by the senior pastor to serve as the Christian education pastor for all ages but was expected by church board members to be the youth pastor. After several months of negotiating with competing groups within the church, I was reassigned to serve as the administrative pastor, which lasted five months. After returning from a family vacation, I was informed that I was being let go because the church could no longer afford to keep me on staff. I had been in the church a total of eighteen months. I was now ready to do anything but serve as a pastor in another church. Although God had called me at age thirteen to give my life to full-time Christian ministry, my experiences indicated that the local church was not as healthy as it could be. My assignments were short-term. I then discovered that my calling was actually to help the local church develop spiritual leaders.

I believe the local church can be better than it is. I believe the local church is spending the majority of its time and energy on things that do not matter in the long run. I believe the local church in America is worried more about keeping programs running than freeing people up to serve as God intended. If leaders in the local church actually assumed responsibility to develop people instead of programs and to give away ministry instead of taking joy away from potential leaders, perhaps more people would want to attend church (Barna 19). The church should be a body of believers where lives are transformed, not a club where people mingle with like-minded individuals. Every church has what it needs to do what God wants it to do. However, not every church takes advantage of what God has provided (Barna 19). Perhaps emerging leaders are sitting in the pews wishing they could participate in what God is doing in the community. A different approach is required in order to bring that potential into reality—one that is different than I have experienced in ten years of pastoral ministry.

Recognizing the Problem

Leaders are in short supply (Forman, Jones, and Miller 23-24; Nees; Malphurs and Mancini 8-9; Barna 18). Every family, company, city, state, and nation needs leaders. Churches crave strong leadership as well. Churches call pastors to lead churches in a certain direction. Other leaders are absent in most churches, which means that pastors have little support in their leadership responsibilities. When pastors move, few laypeople feel capable of holding the reins of leadership. In addition, a lack of spiritual leadership in local churches oftentimes results in poor decisions and missed opportunities. I have seen too many churches simply maintaining what they have or going through a slow death instead of being what God called them to be. As a result, the church and the world suffer. An intentional process of helping potential leaders become godly, spiritual leaders in the church would address the problem. If possessing a plan for leadership development became the norm in local churches, they would make a significant difference in American society (Barna 19-20).

The Church of the Nazarene is becoming aware of this issue. The denomination posted data from "Faith Communities Today: A Survey of Churches of the Nazarene" on its Web site that gives an idea of the state of the local church. It is based on the responses of leaders from 436 randomly selected Nazarene churches. According to that survey, 47 percent of churches have had three or more pastors in the past ten years. With so much transition in leadership, I am not surprised that leaders are unable to develop other leaders. They do not stay in one church long enough to do so. Consequently, every few years, churches experience a void in personnel to ensure that they are staying focused on God's agenda. In addition, 28 percent of churches cannot find enough people willing to serve in the church. A leadership development strategy would help to address this problem as well. The Mid-Atlantic District Church of the Nazarene has been conducting leadership cohorts among pastors for several years to develop them as leaders. Now the district is turning its attention to the development of leaders among the laity (*Moving with God 82-83*).

The laypeople who attend the church through numerous pastoral transitions are seldom equipped for ministry or trained as leaders in the church (Forman, Jones, and Miller 24). Instead, in such churches, only the pastor does the ministry of the church. In some cases, the majority of those who attend weekly worship services are spectators. People attend in order to receive religious good and services (Minatrea 7; Malphus and Mancini 7). They do not know the joy of using their spiritual gifts, strengths, passions, and personality for kingdom building. This example is oftentimes a best-case scenario. Many worst-case scenarios exist as well—churches with poor leadership that simply strive to keep the bills paid and the doors open. They exist but have little to no impact in the community and fail to participate in the mission of God.

The church does not have to operate this way. Although the people in the church may be the church's greatest liability, the people in the church are also the church's greatest resource apart from the Holy Spirit. A church that mobilizes its people to participate in mission can continue along God's agenda whether a pastor is currently at the helm or not. If the laity were trained and equipped as leaders, they could use their God-given strengths to participate in the mission of God in the immediate community and beyond (Bartz 86). A church should disciple new believers so that, in time, the church might also intentionally develop these disciples into spiritual leaders. Although every disciple will not become a leader in the church, a strategy is required to help potential leaders attain the level of spiritual leadership to which God has called them (Huizing 344; West 9). Taking this step would greatly enhance a church's ability to continue the mission of Jesus Christ.

Churches need to identify and grow leaders. However, churches commonly do things a certain way because they have always been done that way, unless a better method of doing things has been tried and proven successful. Many pastors and lay leaders need more information before they would be willing to take the steps necessary to create a leadership development pathway in their church. Perhaps churches could take steps to change current trends if they became aware of what other churches were actually doing and what strategies for leadership development were effective. An in-depth look at a greenhouse church might begin to provide some of these answers.

Chapter One
Start with Story

EVERY BUILDING project begins with a story. The first greenhouse began with a story about Tiberius and cucumbers. Throughout history people have moved to a particular location with a certain history and dream of possibilities before building. The stories they tell reveal the purpose of their building projects. This truth applies to the building of a greenhouse church as well.

In the beginning, God created a story. We refer to it as the Creation story. God is continuing to create stories in people's lives, weaving events and responses of individuals and communities together in dramatic fashion. God is also looking for spiritual leaders in the local church to become co-authors with him. In recent years, God has blessed me by revealing a perspective into the story he is writing in my life. He is calling me to work with him in the development of leaders in the local church. Through insights gained in reading texts and other books, through my experiences and the inspiration of the Holy Spirit, I am beginning to see how this calling should take shape in the real world. One of my favorite questions to bring application from observation and interpretation is, "What will it look like?" My story has revealed that developing leaders in a greenhouse church will look like intentionally focusing on three primary themes: Meditation, Mentoring, and Mission. These are the pillars that support the greenhouse church.

Meditation

Leadership development in the local church begins with meditation. Meditation is the practice of mentally dwelling upon God's instruction, commandments, and promises. The concept of meditation has been taken hostage by New Age philosophy. I am not referring to the idea of transporting one's self to a place of serenity or advocating any use of yoga. Meditation is maintaining an attitude of prayer so that a person may hear from God what is Truth. According to teaching pastor and author John Ortberg, "In a sense, meditation is just positive worry. If you know how to worry, you know how to meditate" (92). He explains that meditation is being in the presence of God in the only way possible—in the mind: "So being *with* God is something that takes place primarily in our thoughts, our mind" (80, italics original). That is why the present is the best moment of my life, for it is the only moment I have to be in the presence of God (62). Therefore, I believe leadership development begins with meditation on the heart of God and his holiness.

Many secular experts on leadership development focus on the right traits or techniques necessary to build leaders. However, the process of leadership development looks different for those called by God to be spiritual leaders. Our starting point must always be God. It is only through divine revelation that we can know who God is and who He calls us to be. Meditation is simply focusing upon His voice to guide us in the present. Author Dallas Willard stated the significance of abiding in Christ's presence rather than depending upon proper techniques:

> The minister does not need tricks and techniques, but need only speak Christ's word from Christ's character, standing within the manifest presence of God. Of course, we are talking about a steady course of life, not a momentary inspiration, and for such a life in its leaders the church languishes. (247)

I am realizing that being a leader in the church is much different than being a leader. The world has a bunch of CEO's and political leaders. However, in order to be faithful to my calling as a spiritual leader in the church, I must maintain right relationship with God. Unless this foundation is secure, everything else is prone to collapse.

I must start leading by looking up and within. According to Earl Creps, "In the end, my best practice must be me" (3). I must daily look up and yield to God's will in my life. I must continually listen for God's voice leading me to his agenda. Then I must look within and align my practices to his will. Calvin Miller terms this practice "centering". He wrote, "Centering is the act of focus in our relationship with God. ... It is from this divine conversation that the church secures both the knowledge of her assignment and the power to accomplish it" (103). Church leaders must examine their lives with the Holy Spirit as their guide to determine what changes are needed to maintain right relationship with God and follow his will.

The rest of my leadership will result as an overflow of meditation. Willard reminded leaders in the church of how character influences leadership:

> And the best gift I can give them [my neighbors] is always *the character and power of Christ in me and in others who really trust him*. Beyond that I look to God for the renovation of their hearts as well. (255, italics original)

Several years ago, another pastor on our district shared a very similar word of wisdom: "The greatest gift you can give anyone is your relationship with Jesus." Meditation upon God's Word and God's will is a prerequisite to developing the character of a leader that is worth following.

This posture of meditation does not apply just to me as the pastor. It applies to all who lead in the church. Therefore, it is my responsibility to teach and to expect that all leaders in the local church must become leaders of the self before they lead anything else. Again, the words of Willard are instructive:

> … they [the leadership of the local congregation] must recognize that the first step in leading the people who are there to become apprentices of Jesus is for the ministering elders and overseerers to *be* apprentices of Jesus. (244, italics original)

The goal of the meditation I am advocating is that leaders would be formed as apprentices of Jesus. Anything less is simply the blind leading the blind. Aubrey Malphurs would agree. He said, "Godly character is *the essential ingredient* that qualifies Christians to lead others" (19, emphasis added). Some may possess ambitions of leadership in the church, but without the necessary qualifications, such leadership will never amount to much. Henry and Richard Blackaby explained why this is so: "People do not choose to become spiritual leaders. Spiritual leadership flows out of a person's vibrant, intimate relationship with God" (100). Mature discipleship precedes leadership in the church. And it must start with me. I must model what that looks like.

Eugene Peterson has modeled for me what spiritual leadership looks like in the local church. In his memoirs he offered this wisdom:

> My "work" assignment was to pay more attention to what God does than what I do and then to find, and guide others to find, the daily, weekly, yearly rhythms that would get this awareness into our bones. (45)

In other words, my role as pastor and spiritual leader requires that I *pay attention*. I meditate upon what God does in me and in our community. In order to "get this awareness into our bones" I must be disciplined in directing my thoughts to God. According to Blackaby, "More than anything else, people are looking for spiritual leaders who are clearly experiencing God's presence" (96). This demands some effort on my part.

I do have a role to play in becoming an authentic apprentice of Jesus. In the past, I have felt guilty for not following a prescribed pattern of journaling, Scripture memorization and devotional reading. Recently, I have discovered a better approach to spiritual growth. Willard explained the tension that exists regarding my role in my spiritual development:

> There are no formulas—no definite how-tos—for growth in the inner character of Jesus. Such growth is a way of relentless seeking. … But there are many things we can do to place ourselves at the disposal of God. (94)

1 Timothy 4:7 says, "… train yourselves to be godly" (NIV). I must enter strict training under the guidance of one who has gone before. Diogenes Allen suggested that such training includes learning to control our passions:

> These theologians [desert monastics] clearly know that the ability to love our neighbors and to love God comes from God, but we can resist and hinder God's grace by our failure to control those desires that awaken our passions. … Those who seek to follow Christ, even though forgiven, are still weak and rebellious in various respects. Unless they *make the effort* to overcome their weaknesses and rebellious attitudes, they will be greatly hampered in their efforts to follow Christ. (67, emphasis added)

To maintain a posture of holiness whereby I can be effective as a spiritual leader, I must meditate upon what passions pull me away from God. I must meditate upon the promises of God, which equip me to overcome temptation and "rebellious attitudes." God will not "deliver me from evil"—as we are taught to pray in the Lord's Prayer—without my desire to actually be delivered. My role is to "take captive every thought to make it obedient to Christ" (2 Cor. 10:5) and allow God to do His work of deliverance.

Another important element of meditation is waiting—waiting upon God. Henri Nouwen related a significant insight from Simone Weil, who said, "Waiting patiently in expectation is the foundation of the spiritual life" (12). Waiting in expectation is an active waiting, but its emphasis is on God's activity rather than upon my activity. This is another discipline I am learning. My months of recuperation from multiple surgeries taught me to wait upon God's healing, strength, and provision. The process has made me a better leader.

This focus upon self (meditating upon my relationship with God, my passions, distractions, etc.) is for a greater purpose. It is not just to make me a better individual. It is to equip me for leadership and leadership development in the church. Meditation upon the word and will of God calls me into God's mission. Creps stated it clearly in reference to 1 Peter 5:3: "A missional perspective springs *from a transformed interior life* that gives us moral authority to lead God's people, "not lording it over those entrusted to you, but *being examples to the flock*" (*Disciplines* 14, emphasis mine). I am learning the significance of being over doing, for the sake of being an example. In the context of leadership development in the local church, this means, "Leadership development has more to do with who they *are* as a church than what particular things they *do*" (Forman, Jones, and Miller, 30, emphasis original). Furthermore, in order to develop leaders, I must first make disciples and mature apprentices of Jesus. Forman, Jones and Miller contend, "We need to seek to bring all to maturity, and then from these maturing people we need to develop many for leadership" (54). They go on to say, "Yet, you can't have mature leaders if you don't have spiritually mature people" (146). That is how it comes full circle: meditation leads to mentoring and leadership development which leads to mission. It is not all about me, but I must start with me.

Mentoring

Once I learn to follow Christ as His apprentice, then I can say along with the apostle Paul, "Follow my example, as I follow the example of Christ" (1 Cor. 11:1). This is where meditation moves me into a position for mentoring others. I cannot lead others where I have not traveled. I must become one worth following. I must abide in the vine and in the love of Jesus in order to bear fruit (see John 15:4-5, 9, 16). Mentoring is a sharing of the overflow of my relationship with God.

Mentoring begins when I accept my role as a leader of followers. I do not lead things; I lead people—people created in the image of God. Although some people become stressed with the demands of ministry—with the constant criticism and unreasonable expectations—I have finally learned that I lead best when I am abiding in the love of Jesus. Susan Muto and Adrian van Kaam explained, "The remedy we choose to relieve tension is not a fake smile or a cheap joke or a binging-out experience, but the pursuit of intimacy with the Lord" (71). For many years of my ministry, I did not focus on mentoring others because I was too busy meeting the expectations of others. This was my primary source of stress in ministry. I felt like I was treated as a commodity rather than a person. I was valued according to what people could get out of me, and I allowed it. However, I am in a new assignment now. I have learned so many valuable lessons through my time of waiting—waiting 10 months for another pastoral assignment after being sabotaged by my church board in Maine—waiting 18 months for another pastoral assignment after hearing that the local church where I served in central Delaware could no longer afford to keep me on staff, and most recently, waiting for 3 months on disability to see if I could be productive at my secular work again. I have learned that who I am is more significant than what I can or cannot change, and that truth should determine how I treat those under my leadership. They are people. Intimacy with God keeps me from losing perspective of this important fact.

I am to love followers the way that Jesus loves (John 13:34, 15:12). Mentoring involves intentionally investing in the lives of disciples and showing them the way forward. Malphurs stated, "If followers are to make an unwavering commitment to Christ, leaders who profess to be committed Christ-followers must lead the way to committed discipleship" (16). Just as young men centuries ago learned trades by working as apprentices under a skilled craftsman, disciples become mature disciples under the guidance of a mature Christ-follower. This means that I must model what mature discipleship looks like in our culture and community. In the context of daily life, I am to pour myself into disciples-in-training as Jesus poured Himself into his disciples.

This is why the church is necessary. We were created for relationship. In the context of the Body of Christ, disciples learn from one another. Nouwen explained, "Christian community is the place where we keep the flame alive among us and take it seriously, so that it can grow and become stronger in us" (12). It is within this community of fellow-disciples that friendships, informal mentoring relationships, and formal mentoring relationships are formed. These are the types of relationships necessary for spiritual growth, as Proverbs 27:17 declares: "As iron sharpens iron, so one person sharpens another."

Friendships are significant. Rowland Forman, Jeff Jones and Bruce Miller helped me understand just how significant friendships are in the church:

> Because mentoring is at its essence a friendship, forcing people into mentoring partnerships seldom works. Rather, we need to hold high the value of intentional

spiritual friendships, model what it means to be a spiritual father or mother, and provide opportunities for God-directed mentor links to take place. (67)

This may occur through small groups or service projects. Whenever I give opportunities for our people to be together and get to know one another, I am providing opportunities for the development of spiritual friendships.

Tremendous potential for spiritual growth exists within the context of the community of believers. In a small group and among friends, we can be honest, accountable, vulnerable, and encouraging to one another. More mature disciples and group leaders can also develop friendships that grow into mentoring relationships with less mature disciples in the group. Another context for mentoring in the local church is among the existing leadership, specifically with the church board. The majority of painful encounters I have experienced in my 17 years of pastoral ministry have stemmed from connection with local church board members. That is why my passion is leadership development in the local church. The problem is that many (if not most) church boards lack strong spiritual leadership. I resonate with the observation of Forman, Jones and Miller:

> Board members are typically well-meaning, but few have ever been mentored for their ministry responsibilities. Rarely has anyone intentionally focused on developing their character, maturity, or their theology, especially their theology of the church. (24)

Oftentimes it is taken for granted that church board members are the spiritually mature members of the congregation. Sadly, this is not always true. Just because someone became elected to a position of leadership in the church does not mean that he/she understands the character qualities or skills needed for the position. Mentoring is one way to intentionally provide opportunities for the spiritual development of church board members and other leaders in the church.

One reason I chose to emphasize mentoring in my leadership development plan for a greenhouse church is that it has not been a part of my church experience in the past. I read about mentoring relationships in Scripture and hear about its benefits; however, I do not see much mentoring taking place in the churches where I have served. Perhaps the reason for this lies in its definition. Again, Forman, Jones and Miller provided help in understanding what mentoring looks like in the church: "Ultimately, leadership development is as simple and organic as one person believing in another and building into his or her life" (31). This is also a helpful starting point for understanding mentoring – "believing in another and building into his or her life." It may be simple, but it is costly. Pouring yourself into another is demanding, time consuming, and sometimes frustrating, which may explain why it is so often avoided.

In fact, leadership development, discipleship, spiritual growth, and mentoring are all very messy. It is a messy business to get involved in the messy lives of others. Michael Yaconelli, author of *Messy Spirituality,* explains the human condition:

> None of us is who we appear to be. We all have secrets. We all have issues. We all struggle from time to time. No one is perfect. Not one. (I have just paraphrased Romans 3:10.) The essence of messy spirituality is the refusal to pretend, to lie, or to allow others to believe we are something we are not. Unfortunately, people can handle the most difficult issues more easily than they can handle the lack of pretending. (27)

These are the people God is calling me to love and mentor into mature discipleship. I must remind people who they really are as children of God. Even though it is a messy business to confront the secrets, the issues, and the lies (in addition to the immaturity, the sins, the apathy, the irresponsibility, the stubbornness, the pride, the confusion, the addictions, the prejudices, the mental models, and the untrustworthiness) present in the lives of individuals, I must remember that Jesus did it for me. I can mentor imperfect people because God loves imperfect people like me.

Jesus is our example. He gathered twelve unschooled, ordinary men together and poured His life and teaching into them. His method was to be with them—to share life *with* them (see Acts 4:13). Jesus (and also the apostle Paul) invested in others in order to build their character. This took priority over learning methods and skills for leadership. In *The Leadership Baton*, Forman, Jones and Miller pointed out, "Both [Jesus and Paul] were effective in mentoring emerging leaders in the context of doing ministry to build competence and sound doctrine. Yet for both, *building character* came first" (45, emphasis original). Therefore, in my mentoring efforts, building character must also be my focus.

I can begin to build character in others by preaching the Word, modeling the Way, and sharing life with life. Jesus, who is the Way, the Truth, and the Life, makes such an audacious dream possible (see John 14:6). Basically, this means preaching the gospel of Jesus, modeling Christlikeness, and sharing life with others as Jesus did. Teaching moments occur in the everyday experiences of life; yet I have to be present to take advantage of them. Therefore, time spent together with followers is vital.

Jesus revealed another lesson regarding mentoring recently. I purchased a gift for someone (a children's Bible) at a Christian bookstore and it was placed in a bag. The bag had a verse on it: "When he saw the crowds, *he had compassion on them*, because they were harassed and helpless, *like sheep without a shepherd*" (Matt. 9:36, emphasis added). This was a reminder that when I look at people, I need to understand what they are feeling; I need to identify with their pain. This is a weakness of mine. I tend to focus on my own thoughts rather than upon the feelings of others. However, if I am to follow Jesus, I must live as He did (see 1 John 2:6). I must follow His example and have compassion on others. The reason is that people are lost—like sheep without a shepherd. They wander around in circles because they lack leadership. People are looking for a leader to point the way through the obstacles of life. That is what I feel God is calling me to do as a mentor and pastor, to care for the sheep by teaching them the way to go. And compassion prompts me to act on their behalf.
Nevertheless, I do not always feel compassionate. Feelings come and go. However, the mission of God never changes. It is the missio dei that provides the ultimate motivation to serve on behalf of the sheep entrusted to my care. It is the missio dei that awakens my soul to see the distance between God's plans for humanity and present reality, and this moves my heart to have compassion upon the sheep that have no shepherd. While meditation upon my relationship with God leads me to mentor those in my sphere of influence, it also brings me near to the heart of God, who loves the world. I meditate and mentor in order to lead people to participate in the mission of God.

Mission

Leadership development in the local church is not about self-improvement for self-improvement's sake. It is for mission. Creps stated, "Rather than drawing people to the center, a missional life means Jesus sending us outward, as the Father sent Him" (*Disciplines* 10). Leaders influence people. Christian leaders influence disciples and equip them to continue the mission of Jesus. I am not trying to build a mega-church by investing in the development of leaders; rather, I am entrusting the teaching of Jesus to reliable individuals who will also be qualified to teach others (see 2 Tim. 2:2). I will send these leaders out into the community to fulfill the mission.

The Greenhouse Church

In order to lead a missional church, I must also focus on being transformational. If being missional gets people outside the walls of the church, that is great, but without transformation in the lives of believers and non-believers, it is incomplete. I, as a missional and transformational leader, must rely upon God to do His work; I cannot transform anyone. Nevertheless, I do have a role to play. Henry and Richard Blackaby explained, "The success of a spiritual leader is not measured in dollars, percentages, numbers, or attendance. A person is truly a spiritual leader when others are moved to be more like Christ" (100). I cannot cause growth to occur, but I can plant and water seeds to facilitate their growth (see 1 Cor. 3:6). Mission and transformation are inseparable elements of the missio dei. That mission has made its way down through the centuries to include me.

I can write stories with God. I can participate in His work as He writes stories in people's lives. I can influence others to live in our culture, but not participate in the humanistic values of our culture. Nouwen pointed out how we can exert this counter-cultural influence:

> The spiritual life is a life in which we wait, actively present to the moment, trusting that new things will happen to us, new things that are far beyond our imagination, fantasy, or prediction. That, indeed, is a very radical stance toward life in a world preoccupied with control. (11)

Those who fight to maintain control of their lives will notice our stance. The peace that characterizes our approach to each day will be attractive to those watching and stressing over present circumstances and future uncertainties. I know this because people have told me how my calm demeanor is appreciated in the public high school where I work. On a Christmas card one administrator wrote, "Your calm way of handling things makes me wish I could be just like you!" My trust in God, my spiritual life, and my waiting enable me to *be* engaged in mission around the clock.

Another way to focus on our mission is to focus upon self-control. Allen made it clear that we cannot reach out in mission until we first sacrifice selfish desires:

> … if we cannot control our appetites, it is unlikely that we can ever be strong enough to give up anything for the sake of another person or do something for the sake of another when it runs counter to one of our appetites. Loving our neighbor as ourselves will always be out of our reach. (68)

The Greenhouse Church

I have experienced that many Christians in churches think that they can have the best of both worlds. They can live for God and participate in His mission while doing whatever they want. If I am going to be successful at developing leaders in the local church who are living reminders of God's heartbeat in the world, I must model and teach self-sacrifice and self-control first. That is why I chose to focus on meditation before mentoring and mission. Meditating on my own need for gratification will open my heart to God's Spirit who provides strength to overcome temptation. This lesson must also be taught to those I mentor. Then leaders-in-training will understand that mission is an overflow of what they have experienced first-hand.

Reaching out in mission is an act of love. God's love is costly. In order to love another, I have to give of myself. Love is breathing life into another. Unless I am constantly being filled with the love of God, I will eventually run out of love for others. Then the mission will truly be mission impossible.

If I start leading a church to participate in God's mission without ensuring that believers have a growing relationship with God, all of our efforts will simply amount to good works. Author Milfred Minatrea explained, "... passion is kindled only in the midst of a white-hot love relationship with God. Knowing Him, His heart, yields passion. Pursuing what is on His heart informs practice" (25-26). Pursuing a passion for the lost begins with a passion for knowing the heart of God. When the disciples informed Jesus that the crowds were seeking for Him, Jesus did not concede to their expectations. Instead, he went elsewhere. He was pursuing the mission of God but doing so according to the directives received through time spent with His Father (see Mark 1:35-38). I am called to follow the example of Jesus.

At one time, I served as a leader in a church plant and also served at the public high school where I worked as a technology specialist. My mission was the same in both environments. Malphurs explained the role Christian leaders are to serve both within the church and also outside the walls of the church:

> In a church or parachurch ministry, leaders not only serve by leading the church in some capacity, but they also model Christlikeness. ... In the non-Christian or not-necessarily-Christian context, Christians are Christian leaders as well. They serve as "salt and light" people (Mt. 5:13-16) to those around them who may or may not know the Savior. (13-14)

I modeled Christlikeness whether I was in the church or whether I was serving the staff in the public high school. Christlikeness is basically what it means to live a holy life. Holiness, therefore, along with transformation, active waiting, self-control, and knowing the heart of God, is a necessary element of mission.

Leadership development in a greenhouse church will cause people to draw closer to God, so they can actively participate in His mission. Programs, even mission programs, are not a substitute for one's hunger and thirst for God. Minatrea declared, "Without the exposure to the missionary passion of God, members may learn about opportunities and ongoing mission ministry, but lack the heart of God, which moves that knowledge to action" (147). Mission work devoid of this passion that flows from the heart of God is not transformative. It is simply work. I know several good people that do-good things, but they are not participating in the mission of God because they have no relationship with him. I also know individuals who claim to be Christ-followers and desire to travel in the name of Christ and do mission work; however, their walk does not match their testimony. This practice also is not participation in the mission of God. Minatrea pointed out, "Transformed believers can transform society" (137). This is because God is at work in the lives of transformed believers. God is also already at work in the world, but for me to participate in that work, I have to stay close to the God of mission.

My prayer is that I will not get distracted by lesser things. As I develop spiritual leaders and teach about meditation, mentoring, and mission, I want to keep my heart where it belongs. John Wesley wrote about Christian perfection, and I see this as the foundation of leadership development in the local church:

> … I saw, in a clearer and clearer light, the indispensable necessity of having "the mind which was in Christ," and of "walking as Christ also walked;" even of having, not some part only, but all the mind which was in Him; and of walking as He walked, not only in many or in most respects, but in all things. … This is the way wherein those children of God once walked, who being dead still speak to us: 'Desire not to live but to praise His name; let all your thoughts, words, and works tend to His glory.' 'Let your soul be filled with so entire a love to Him, that you may love nothing but for His sake.' 'Have a pure intention of heart, a steadfast regard to His glory in all our actions.' (11, 13)

After reading Wesley's *A Plain Account of Christian Perfection* the first time, I wrote this note in the back of my Bible:

> Today is Mon. Jan. 18, 1993. God is doing a new thing in my life. I want to know Christ and the pain of suffering with him and the power of the resurrection. I want to pray continually. ... Here I am Lord, use me! I'm yours! Take all of me. I die to myself today. I no longer want to meet my own desires, but only the desire to know and love you more. ... Father hear my cry, my plea—this is my heart's desire. By your grace alone, please allow me to live a life worthy of the calling you have given me—both now and forevermore I pray. Amen.

This is still the cry of my heart. I have experienced a lot since I wrote those words, but I still mean them. They mean more to me now. God has been faithful and answered my prayer. He has taken me down many rough roads. The journey has taught me to trust Him and to love Him more.

God is writing an amazing story in my life and in the lives of future leaders in my sphere of influence. As I develop leaders—as I meditate, mentor, and engage in God's mission—my prayer continues to be, "Please allow me to live a life worthy of the calling you have given me." That calling is to keep co-writing with God. The stories we are writing are masterpieces, but they aren't finished yet.

Questions for reflection or discussion:

1. What are the highlights of your story?
2. How is God shaping you?
3. What do you think of the practice of meditation as it was defined in this chapter?
4. How can meditation help church leaders abide in Christ?
5. What mentors have you had in the past?
6. Where do you look for mentors?
7. How can mentoring influence the existing lay leadership development strategy in your church?
8. What is your mission in one sentence?
9. What do you appreciate about the story God is writing in your life?
10. How can you be a co-author with God in writing stories in others?

Chapter Two
Understanding Your Role

PEOPLE NEED help in order to grow. Although attending church services is important, merely passing through the turnstiles of the church each week and filling a spot on a pew will not result in transformation. Church leaders have a role to play in the development of emerging leaders. Gardeners must maintain oversight of plants and regulate the temperature, humidity, and ventilation in greenhouses. They also eliminate threats to the plants' health. Pastors and existing leaders within a local church must likewise maintain oversight of growing believers. They must also regulate the church climate and eliminate potential threats to lay leadership development.

When local church leaders do not understand their role in the development of others, few church leaders are formed. This is a problem. Intentional and effective lay leadership development practices remain nonexistent in many congregations despite the need for strong spiritual leadership in America's Christian churches, the frequent turnover of pastoral leadership, and access to high-quality leadership resources via the Internet. Christians have lamented for years that more and more churches are closing their doors, church attendance rates cannot keep up with population growth rates, and morality in America is steadily declining. In addition to these troubling cultural trends, the current average tenure for US and Canadian pastors in the Church of the Nazarene is six years and two months (Lance). This statistic means that local churches without strong lay leadership essentially reinvent themselves every five to seven years. Leadership development materials abound in the worlds of business and academia but have not resourced emerging leaders in most American Christian churches. Numerous books, articles, and organizations exist to facilitate the development of future leaders; however, based upon my experience, relatively few church leaders take advantage of these channels.

The reasons behind these observations remain a mystery. People may observe that pastors are busy and churches have other priorities, but perhaps more to the story remains to be discovered. Conjecture also does little to move church leaders toward workable solutions. Therefore, after surveying the landscape of lay leadership development literature, I probed current reality concerning leadership development issues in a sample of local churches. Through the process of asking the right questions, I shed light on some possible answers and discovered workable strategies for lay leadership development in the local church. The purpose of my research was to obtain information for the formation of effective lay leadership development strategies in local churches by discovering the current lay leadership development strategies of pastors and the relationship of these strategies to the perspectives obtained from church lay leaders.

Theological Framework

The pastor's role includes understanding the theological framework that shapes lay leadership development strategies. This theological framework along with biblical norms concerning leadership development inform leadership development theories and practices that should be applied to each local church's unique context. God has revealed himself as Father, Son, and Holy Spirit—the Triune God; therefore, an appropriate theology of leadership development must reflect the three-in-one nature of God. Stephen A. Seamands writes, "The ministry we have entered is the ministry *of* Jesus Christ, the Son, *to* the Father, *through* the Holy Spirit, *for* the sake of the church and the world" (original emphasis; 9-10). This observation provides a solid foundation upon which one may build a theology of ministry and, more specifically, a theology of leadership development in the local church. Rather than serving the purposes of one individual, lay leadership development builds others up so that God is glorified. The mission of Jesus determines the agenda for lay leadership development strategies. That assignment has been entrusted to believers and can only be accomplished by the power of the Holy Spirit. Each Person in the Trinity models essential components that combine to form biblical lay leadership development strategies.

Leadership Development as the Ministry of Jesus Christ, the Son

God intends for all believers to reflect the love and grace of Jesus Christ. Followers of Christ are to follow in the footsteps of Jesus and to live as he lived. The church exists in order to continue the work and ministry in which Jesus was consumed while he walked upon the earth. Jesus set an example for loving sacrificially, praying sincerely, and forgiving completely. He also demonstrated the way mature disciples should develop church leaders.

Business models of leadership and leadership development have provided some help to the modern Christian church, but they must not serve as the church's agenda. John R. W. Stott observes, "Our model of leadership is often shaped more by culture than by Christ. Yet many cultural models of leadership are incompatible with the servant imagery taught and exhibited by the Lord Jesus" (113). This mistake illustrates why a correct foundation is essential for the church's ministry; the direction an individual is heading when he or she takes his or her first step determines the course that lies ahead. Churches follow this law as well, unless of course, churches make midcourse corrections. Church leaders who are attempting to follow in the footsteps of Jesus are still prone to reflect the ideals of culture rather than reflect the image of God in Christ. This tendency must be met by the reiteration and internalization of the mission of Jesus.

Jesus' mission was to create a community that would incarnate the gospel message in the world. In order to accomplish his mission, Jesus chose to forgo the shortcuts of impressing people with magic tricks, taking advantage of his divinity, or thinking primarily of himself (see Matt. 4:1-11). Instead, he chose a different method:

> [A] community was created in which the embodiment of [his] mission continued corporately after his ascension, as a household, a family, a community, *koinonia*.... This runs against the premise that the church is essentially an impersonal, imposed, hierarchal organization of offices and officers. (Oden, *Life in the Spirit* 280)

The Christian church is not a business. It is a fellowship of disciples on a mission—the mission of Jesus Christ.

Jesus created this missional community, not by following a formula or curricula but by inviting people to a shared life (Ford 200). According to Leighton Ford, "that, in a nutshell, is what Jesus did to develop his leaders: He gave them himself" (221). He spent time with his disciples. He lived with them so that they had a proper vantage point to notice how he related to people. Thomas C. Oden states, "The training of the Twelve occurred didactically and experientially by proximate association with him [Jesus]. They listened to him teach and watched him respond to human need and deal with adversaries. They beheld his steady compassion" (*Word of Life* 296). Jesus did have a plan to accomplish his mission, but it was not popular, trendy, or painless. Ford explains, "Jesus had a strategy to develop leaders—he aimed to reproduce himself in them" (221). Rather than learning to follow a lesson plan or a certain protocol, the disciples were learning to follow a person.

That strategy is illustrated throughout the Gospels, as Jesus called his disciples to do what he did and to communicate his love to others. In the final hours before his arrest, Jesus revealed his intentions clearly to those closest to him:

- "I have set you an example that you should do as I have done for you" (John 13:15).

- "A new command I give you: Love one another. As I have loved you, so you must love one another" (John 13:34).
- "If you obey my commands, you will remain in my love, just as I have obeyed my Father's commands and remain in his love" (John 15:10).
- "My command is this: Love each other as I have loved you" (John 15:12).

Paul summarized this plan—this mission of God—as he told the believers in Ephesus to imitate God and the love of Jesus (Eph. 5:1-2). As dearly loved children, they were expected to reflect a family resemblance to the Father and the Son. A committed disciple is one who follows in the footsteps of Jesus and learns to love as he loves. Aubrey Malphurs and Will Mancini share that the three main characteristics of true disciples are that they abide in his Word (John 8:31-32), love one another (John 13:34-35), and bear fruit (John 15:8, 16; 65). In order to develop leaders in the local church, a leader must intentionally work with God to make disciples who obey God's Word, love selflessly and sacrificially as Jesus did, and engage in the painstaking work of making other disciples. To love like Christ is to risk getting hurt. Brennan Manning expresses this point: "Those who wear bulletproof vests protecting themselves from failure, shipwreck, and heartbreak will never know what love is. The unwounded life bears no resemblance to the Rabbi" (158). Investing in the lives of others means taking risks and sometimes being wounded.

Loving like Jesus also requires a firsthand experience of his love: "One can follow Jesus' example only if one has already experienced Jesus' loving service for oneself" (O'Day 727). Manning agrees: "If I am not in touch with my own belovedness, then I cannot touch the sacredness of others.... Being accepted, enamored, and loved by God comes first, motivating the disciple to live the law of love" (58, 83). Contemporary Christian churches may invest in helping people discover their spiritual gifts and personality types through a variety of inventories; however, what churches really need may be inventories to determine their capacity to love. According to John 13:35, "By this all men will know that you are my disciples, if you love one another." Individuals who are abiding in the love of Jesus are in the best position to influence others for the sake of the kingdom.

Jesus purposefully invested in his disciples and taught them to love as he did so that they could continue his mission. Jesus did not worry about leadership development. He was more concerned about creating a community that knew the meaning of loving unconditionally. In the process, he focused on twelve disciples. Moreover, in raising up twelve disciples, he actually poured more of himself into Peter, James, and John. Jesus invested in potential leaders:

> He [Jesus] knew that some people were more willing to receive his teaching and to act upon it than were others. Some were more prepared to understand deep truths than others did. By investing in small groups such as the twelve disciples, Jesus was preparing for the day when people like Peter would be powerful leaders themselves. (Blackaby and Blackaby 219)

Likewise, spiritual leaders today should ask God for discernment to discover in whom they should invest themselves. This inquiry is part of the overall process of developing leaders as Jesus did. According to Malphurs and Mancini, Jesus performed four basic steps to move people from casual observers to committed leaders: (1) He *recruited* disciples who would spend time with him and come to believe in him; (2) he *selected* a committed core into whom he poured his life after spending a night in prayer; (3) he *trained* these twelve disciples through parables, teaching moments, and real experience sharing his ministry; and (4) he *sent them out* to continue his work (63-72). To follow the example of Jesus is a believer's call and privilege. Christians participate in his ongoing ministry by developing leaders as he did.

Leadership Development to the Father

Jesus confessed that his ministry was for the glory of his Father. For example, the Gospel of John reveals why Jesus did what he did:

- John 8:50 declares Jesus' words, "I am not seeking glory for myself; but there is one who seeks it, and he is the judge."
- "Jesus replied, 'If I glorify myself, my glory means nothing. My Father, whom you claim as your God, is the one who glorifies me'" (John 8:54).
- Prior to raising Lazarus from the dead, Jesus prophesied, "This sickness will not end in death. No, it is for God's glory so that God's Son may be glorified through it" (John 11:4b).
- With the disciples in the upper room, Jesus taught, "And I will do whatever you ask in my name, so that the Son may bring glory to the Father" (John 14:13).
- Finally, in John 17 Jesus prayed, "I have brought you glory on earth by completing the work you gave me to do" (v. 4).

The Greenhouse Church

The Son did not selfishly cling to his position of glory but became human; lived among men, women, and children; and, died on the cross to honor his Father. Jesus' desire to glorify the Father best exemplifies his glory.

Jesus could have chosen a different path. He could have lived to fulfill the expectations of needy people; however, Jesus was not driven by the wishes of others. Mark recounted in his gospel an episode when Jesus stayed true to his mission rather than increasing his popularity among the masses:

> Simon and his companions went to look for him, and when they found him, they exclaimed: "Everyone is looking for you!" Jesus replied, "Let us go somewhere else—to the nearby villages—so I can preach there also. That is why I have come." So, he traveled throughout Galilee, preaching in their synagogues and driving out demons. (Mark 1:36-39)

This scene presents another example for disciples and leaders to follow. The expectations of "squeaky wheels" must not set the church leader's agenda.

Spiritual leaders must lead and develop leaders for no other reason than to glorify the Father. Reggie McNeal compares Jesus' response to that of many contemporary leaders:

> Many Christian leaders thrill to hear, "Everyone is looking for you!" Living for the crowd, they die to their mission. Living only for the crowd eventually leaves them emotionally burned-out and empty.... They may claim that their failure is due to having too large a heart for people. This is a self-delusion. The problem is not having a heart *large enough* for God. (original emphasis; *A Work of Heart* 59)

God must set the agenda. The greatest command is to "*Love the Lord your God* with *all* your heart and with *all* your soul and with *all* your mind" (emphasis mine; Matt. 22:37). Contrary to the ways of prevailing culture, this command even applies to those in leadership positions. Ford explains what separates servant-leadership from the popular understanding of leadership:

> Whatever our career may be, true leadership means to receive power from God and to use it under God's rule to serve people in God's way.... The heart of leadership is not in mastering the "how-tos," but in being mastered by the amazing grace of God. (76)

This requirement for Christian leadership is the only way to reflect his love to followers.

The first step to becoming a spiritual leader that develops other leaders involves meditation. Meditation is the practice of reflecting upon God's word. When leaders in the church consider how their lives align with God's expectations, they are better equipped to lead people for the glory of God. The call to abide in Christ (John 15:1-12) finds expression when leaders practice the spiritual discipline of listening to God and meditating upon his promises. Meditation provides strength to Christian leaders and also places them in the proper posture for leadership development.

Meditation also helps leaders understand that success in God's kingdom is different from success in the eyes of the world. Brian Dodd describes what distinguishes these competing value systems:

> The lure of success is seductive. Its siren song causes so many people to uncritically ascribe so much authority to high-profile leaders, platform speakers, and megachurch pastors.... In the United States, this high value placed on success is alien to the value the kingdom of God places on faithfulness and obedience. (11)

Spiritual leaders must redefine success. They must develop leaders who thirst for God, not for power and *success*. In *Practicing Greatness* McNeal instructs, "Great leaders feel profound gratitude to God for their opportunity to give their lives to the mission he has chosen for them. Practicing excellence for them is part of their grateful response to him" (94). Great leaders pursue excellence because they are pursuing intimacy with a great God. According to McNeal, spiritual leaders head toward an uncommon goal:

> Genuinely great spiritual leaders do not do what they do for themselves or even as a way to become recognized as great leaders. The end game for spiritual leaders is about expanding the kingdom of God. They pursue greatness because they are passionate about God and about helping other people experience the life God intended for them to enjoy. In the end, great spiritual leaders are not interested in calling attention to themselves. They point people to a great God. This is the sort of greatness we are desperate for. (8)

The world would look quite differently if the majority of church leaders adopted this view of success.

Leadership development for the glory of God focuses on abiding in the love of God. Blackaby and Blackaby state, "Leadership development comes through character development, because leadership is a character issue" (53). Later they add, "People do not choose to become spiritual leaders. Spiritual leadership flows out of a person's vibrant, intimate relationship with God" (100). When disciples become captivated by the love of God and long to fulfill their purpose of bearing fruit (sharing his love), they are enrolled in God's program of leadership development. Moreover, he alone receives the glory.

Leadership Development through the Holy Spirit

The Holy Spirit influenced Jesus throughout his ministry. The Holy Spirit played a role in his birth (Matt. 1:20) and prompted him to enter the wilderness where he was tempted (Matt. 4:1). Upon his baptism the Holy Spirit descended upon Jesus like a dove (Luke 3:22). Jesus was able to fulfill his mission through the power of the Holy Spirit (Heb. 9:14). Followers of Jesus must likewise remain sensitive to the leading of the Holy Spirit and receive power from the Spirit to continue the ministry of Jesus. Andrew Purves states, "By the work of the Holy Spirit we are joined to Christ's mission from and to the Father, thereby to share in his ministry" (1). The Holy Spirit provides what church leaders need to continue the mission of Jesus.

Leaders have spiritual gifts and natural abilities provided by God; however, apart from an ongoing relationship with Jesus they amount to nothing (John 15:1-5). The Holy Spirit makes this relationship possible (John 14:26, 16:7-14). Reliance upon individual strengths to lead the church does not align with the mission or example of Jesus. Although American culture prizes independence, Jesus modeled dependence upon the Holy Spirit (John 14:10; Acts 1:1-2; Heb. 9:14). Leadership development in the church is a work of the Holy Spirit and cannot succeed without his guidance. Christian leaders need to be mentored by the Holy Spirit before they are qualified to mentor others.

The role of the leader is to maintain right relationship with God. Through prayer and meditation upon God's Word, among other disciplines, leaders may learn to "keep in step with the Spirit" (Gal. 5:25). Leaders offer their God-given passion, spiritual gifts, and personality back to God for use in his service. All personality types are welcome in God's kingdom service. Oden declares, "The Spirit works amid different personal temperaments" (*Life in the Spirit* 203). Christians, therefore, offer themselves as vessels that God can use for his glory.

Consequently, leadership development includes learning to hear God's voice and living in the power of the Spirit. Forman, Jones, and Miller pose this question: "How can we provide a rich context where whole-life development can take place?" (65). The authors go on to provide a theological understanding of the process at work:

> In one sense, *we* don't develop leaders; God does. By his Holy Spirit, he trains, shapes, and molds his leaders. But we can provide an interlocking framework (rather than a formula) to optimize the development of the leaders in whose lives God is working. (original emphasis; 65)

Church leaders can learn to cooperate with God in the leadership development process. They can help guide people into an appropriate posture where the Holy Spirit can act.

The world has dramatically changed since Jesus empowered twelve disciples over two thousand years ago. The mission of Jesus has not changed, but the means to accomplish that task changes with the context. Some churches have turned to business models of leadership in order to meet the challenges of the institutionalized church. The result of substituting the power of the Holy Spirit with knowledge obtained from experts in the business world is a church that resembles a whitewashed tomb. In order to address the complexity of the current context, church leaders must learn to rely upon the direction offered by the Holy Spirit.

The apostle Paul was an effective leader because of his trust in the authority and power of the Holy Spirit. Passages such as Romans 15:18-19 and 1 Corinthians 2:1-5 attest to Paul's dependence upon the Holy Spirit. Dodd notes, "The Holy Spirit is the key to Paul's success.... God takes ordinary people and breathes his Spirit into them, and they accomplish amazing things. But God chooses whom, when and where to blow his Spirit" (24). Neither leaders nor churches can program or manage the Holy Spirit. Christians must submit to his leadership. Dodd also explains that Paul did not refer to his weakness (1 Cor. 2:1-5) to make excuses or display false humility. He adds how an appropriate dependence upon the Holy Spirit should be displayed:

> It is not an invitation to suppress our God-given personality, to pretend we feel weak when we do not or to cultivate a fake frailty.... In other words, the power in every power encounter is in the cross of Christ (for content) and in the Holy Spirit (for communication), irrespective of the weakness of the evangelist. (49-50)

Church leaders must understand that their power to preach the cross of Christ comes only through the Spirit of Christ.

Jesus told his disciples, "Do not leave Jerusalem, but wait for the gift my Father promised, which you have heard me speak about. For John baptized with water, but in a few days you will be baptized with the Holy Spirit" (Acts 1:4-5). The disciples could not fulfill the Great Commission without the strength of the promised Holy Spirit. This divine energy is nothing less than the power that raised Jesus from the dead—the power of the resurrection. This might is available to Jesus' disciples through his Spirit. Gail O'Day explains, "When the church celebrates the beginning of its mission and its empowerment with the Spirit, it also celebrates Easter" (847-48). In Philippians 3:10 Paul prayed, "I want to know Christ and the *power of his resurrection* and the fellowship of sharing in his sufferings, becoming like him in his death" (emphasis mine). This prayer should become the prayer of believers today as well.

Leadership development in the local church exists by the power of the Holy Spirit. The Spirit of Christ calls, equips, empowers, and transforms. The spiritual leader who seeks to develop others as leaders must do so by relying upon the transforming work of the Spirit in the life of the emerging leader.

Significance and Implications of Theological Framework

Leaders can build lay leadership development strategies on the foundation provided by continuing the ministry of the Son, to the Father, through the Holy Spirit. The key pillars are meditation, mentoring, and mission. These supporting practices summarize the role of each person in the Trinity in the formation of leaders through lay leadership development strategies.

Meditation refers to the leader's posture before God the Father. It ensures that the leader's service is done for the glory of God instead of for personal gain. Meditation keeps the leader's mind and heart near to the heart of God. Before a Christian leader can effectively lead other disciples, he or she must be a good follower of God. Meditation is a discipline that makes effective followership possible.

Mentoring refers to the transfer of knowledge through significant relationships. It is most effective when patterned after the work of the Holy Spirit, who teaches people how to apply the teachings of Jesus. Leadership development cannot occur without relationships. However, as a leader partners with the Holy Spirit in the transfer of knowledge to emerging leaders, God is granted space to work in and through the mentoring relationship. That dynamic ultimately leads to transformation and growth in both the mentor and the emerging leader being mentored.

Mission refers to the heart of Jesus' ministry. The purpose of effective lay leadership development is to continue the mission of Jesus, who came for the sick rather than for the righteous (Luke 5:29-32). The mission of the local church is to continue the work and ministry of Jesus as facilitated through effective lay leadership development. Personal and professional development are worthy pursuits; however, when they are detached from the goal of furthering the mission of Jesus, they lose all meaning. A Trinitarian framework for lay leadership development keeps meditation, mentoring, and mission at the center of its strategy and establishes a means for measuring effectiveness.

Leadership Development Strategies in Scripture

A survey of Scripture reveals several norms for leadership development despite lacking a focal section with specific commandments on how local churches must proceed with lay leadership development. The contexts of the Old and New Testaments are different from those of twenty-first century churches, and organized churches did not exist in Scripture until after Pentecost. Even so, lessons may be learned from the pages of the Bible concerning lay leadership development strategies for today's local churches.

Leadership Development in the Old Testament

God was the primary developer of leaders in the Old Testament. He continues to be the primary developer of leaders for the church today (J. Clinton, "Leadership Development Theory" 16-103; McNeal, *Work of Heart* 71-192). By understanding how God developed leaders in Scripture, leaders in the church can then partner with God and help laypeople understand how God may be preparing them for leadership. For example, in Genesis, Noah and Abraham were tested and each responded with obedience (von Rad 120). God told Noah to build an ark on dry land. God chose Abraham to be the father of many nations and yet told him to offer his son as a sacrifice. Joseph faced adversity and flattery and could have responded any number of ways. However, these great leaders placed their trust in God and in his plans. They cooperated with God's initiative and agenda. God selected them to lead his people and gave them instructions or a difficult situation to endure, and they usually responded by doing what was right.

Likewise, God selected Moses to become a leader for the nation of Israel. Moses was an unwilling spokesperson in whom God saw potential. His upbringing in Egypt uniquely qualified him to stand in the gap between Pharaoh and the Jewish slaves. God orchestrated the events in Moses' life to prepare him for leadership (McNeal, *Work of Heart* 6). God also allowed conflict in Moses' life journey, fueling a passion within Moses for justice. Due to his awareness of his weaknesses and his lack of community, Moses became dependent upon God (13). The experiences of his life and uniquely personal encounters with God taught Moses lessons for leadership that he ultimately passed on to his successor, Joshua.

Joshua was Moses' assistant (Exod. 24:13). He accompanied Moses partway up Mt. Sinai, remained in the tent where Moses met with God, heard the call to lead Israel into the Promised Land, and received wisdom at the laying of Moses' hands upon him (Exod. 32:17; 33:11; Deut. 31:7-8; 34:9). For years, Joshua walked in the footsteps of Moses and learned how God works in and through leaders. He also received instruction from his mentor. An account in Numbers 11:28-30 reveals how Moses taught Joshua about humility. Moses demonstrated that leaders should not jealously guard gifts from God such as prophecy but welcome their presence among the masses. The relationship between Moses and Joshua was ordained by God as a means for Joshua's encouragement and strengthening for his future leadership responsibilities (Deut. 3:28).

God took the initiative in the development of David as well. David was not an obvious selection for leadership. His anointing by Samuel took everyone by surprise and set the tone for David's leadership development. God is the author of David's story and does not rely upon outward appearance or physical traits to determine a person's potential. In a similar fashion, David did not always do what was expected, nor was he motivated by the expectations of others (McNeal, *Work of Heart* 26). Furthermore, he made mistakes and learned firsthand of God's grace, which he in turn passed on to others (e.g., 2 Sam. 9). God had a plan for David and called him into leadership. David responded to God's initiative and grew to become whom God knew him to be—a man after God's own heart (e.g., 2 Sam. 7:8; Acts 13:22; 1 Kings 14:8). David's leadership set the standard for greatness for other kings in the Old Testament who followed him.

Leadership Development in the Ministry of Jesus

Spiritual leadership was redefined when a descendant of King David was born in a stable in Bethlehem. Jesus, as fully divine and fully human, demonstrated how to participate in what

God is doing in human lives. God, through Jesus and the work of the Holy Spirit, turned unschooled, ordinary men into fishers of people who changed the world. Although Jesus did not follow a formal leadership development strategy, he did walk in obedience to God and followed God's plan for the spreading of the gospel, which resulted in leaders being developed.

Jesus invited people to get to know him, to believe in him, and then selected a group of believers in whom to invest. He shared life with them and allowed them to participate in his ministry. He took risks by giving ministry away. Although the disciples did not always have success, they learned through the process of failure, teaching, and reflection (e.g., Matt. 17:14-21). The disciples deserted Jesus upon his arrest and Peter disowned him; however, knowing this faintheartedness would occur, Jesus loved them to the end (John 13:1). The Father entrusted the disciples to Jesus (John 17:6-8); the mission of Jesus was the mission of God. Therefore, he did not feel threatened by the process of developing leaders or feel the need to accept personal recognition for any achievements. Jesus did not own the mission; he simply was a leader who, first and foremost, was a great follower (John 14:10; 17:4). Günter Krallmann states, "[B]y training good followers he actually raised outstanding leaders who, once ignited, enlightened and invigorated by the Holy Spirit, turned into excellent achievers for their Lord" (128). Without contemporary leadership development theory or language, Jesus modeled how existing leaders may develop emerging lay leaders in the church.

Jesus' teaching also affirmed the significance of leadership development. For example, John 15:1-17 presents an invitation and a promise. The invitation was to abide in Christ and in his love. The promise was that those who did so would bear fruit; they would know joy and see their prayers answered. Jesus' message to his disciples was a gift—his presence to give them life and power for their mission. They did not have to rely on their own strength or efforts. Jesus gave his emerging leaders the key to discipleship and the fulfillment of mission. This passage is foundational for discipleship and leadership development in the Church. Choosing to abide in Christ and to love as Christ loved sets the stage for the rest of one's spiritual growth and potential development as a leader in the church.

Leadership Development in the Ministry of Paul

Paul may not have literally walked with Jesus and heard his teaching firsthand, but he did learn to walk in Christ's ways. Paul hoped that all people would come to know the transforming power of God and fulfill God's call upon their lives (Acts 26:29; 1 Cor. 9:21-

23; Eph. 4:1). Not only did he seek growth in his own life (Phil. 3:10-14), but he also challenged people to grow. He prayed that believers would grow in the knowledge of God (Col. 1:9-10). He taught that Christ gave apostles, prophets, evangelists, pastors, and teachers to the church "to equip his people for works of service, so that the body of Christ may be built up" (Eph. 4:12). The goal was unity and maturity among the faithful (Eph. 4:13). Paul desired for people to repent, grow in grace and knowledge, and fulfill their calling.

Paul was an early Church leader who helped develop other leaders. His strategy paralleled that of Jesus: (1) Both Jesus and Paul developed leaders in the midst of doing ministry; (2) each focused on godly character; (3) each taught a small team; (4) each provided space for reflection on ministry; and (5) both Jesus and Paul personally invested in mentoring relationships that were more concerned with growth in faithfulness and obedience than in knowledge and skill (Forman, Jones, and Miller 45). As Paul obeyed God and followed in the footsteps of Jesus, he also set an example for believers to follow (Phil. 3:17-21; 1 Cor. 11:1). He took Timothy under his wing and wrote letters to encourage and advise him. When considering candidates for leadership in the church, Paul advised his protégés that potential leaders must have certain character qualities. Dan VanderLugt and Kurt DeHaan summarize 1 Timothy 3:1-13 and Titus 1:6-9 by saying that a church leader "*must* possess: (1) a good reputation, (2) self-control, (3) godly values, (4) a loving heart, (5) a healthy home, (6) a mature faith, and (7) a teachable mind" (original emphasis; 8). Paul hoped that investment in people with these character qualities would cause leaders such as Timothy to emerge.

Perhaps the closest Paul came to articulating his leadership development strategy is found in 2 Timothy 2:2: "And the things you have heard me say in the presence of many witnesses entrust to reliable people who will also be qualified to teach others." Paul did not specify exactly how churches should accomplish or implement this command; however, the goal was clear. Personal development serves to benefit others—specifically, those who learn from existing leaders. By carefully selecting potential leaders with the character qualities he mentioned, Timothy and future leaders could begin to invest in those who would continue to develop as leaders for the church. In 1 Corinthians 3:1-3, Paul lamented over the fact that believers were still "infants in Christ." God does not intend believers to remain immature (Eph. 4:13-15). Therefore, Paul admonished Timothy to give careful attention to the spiritual growth and leadership development of fellow disciples of Jesus.

Leadership Development Theory

The principles found in Scripture continue to guide Christians and spiritual leaders in the twenty-first century. In addition, God still speaks to those with ears to hear, and his Spirit persists in guiding the application of God's Word. Scholars and researchers have sought to understand how God's unchanging purposes find appropriate application in rapidly changing contexts. As a result, the Christian church benefits from their work concerning leadership development theory.

Emergence theory refers to the gradual uncovering of potentialities and the growth in individuals in response to certain events and interpersonal interactions. Rather than adopting views that leaders are born or made, emergent theorists' value what both camps contribute to the understanding of leadership development. They contend, "Leadership can emerge within individuals and organizations in certain environments" (Cenac 126). Followers of Christ may facilitate this growth by responding appropriately to God's initiative as he orchestrates events in the lives of emerging leaders.

According to James Robert Clinton, leadership development is a lifelong process of building upon leadership experiences unique to each individual ("Leadership Development Theory" 16). His proposed formula for emerging leaders is $L=f(p,t,r)$ where L stands for leadership development, f means "a function of," p is processing, t is time, and r is leader response (83). Clinton's son, Richard W. Clinton, explains *processing* as an understanding of God's shaping activity in areas of spiritual formation, ministerial formation, and strategic formation. *Time* analysis refers to the developmental phases leaders go through during their lifetime, and *response* signifies how leaders respond to God's interventions (13-18). If existing leaders understand this process of leadership development, they may guide future leaders and help them to see what God is doing in their lives.

From the outset, spiritual leaders must understand that God will not call everyone to responsibilities of leadership. Discipleship must precede leadership development, but they are not the same thing (Huizing 344). Leaders in the church must keep in mind the difference between discipleship and leadership development when recruiting future leaders. J. R. Woodward explains how some disciples become leaders that develop other leaders:

> We are all players. But we are also all coaches in the sense that we encourage and equip our fellow teammates. But over time, some people, due to their sense of calling, character, influence, experience, gifting and the work of the Holy Spirit, start

to spend more time coaching or equipping other players. And these people are recognized or commissioned as equippers (elders). (198)

All new believers should grow and mature as disciples, but God will call some to take on leadership responsibilities (Malphurs and Mancini 34). The role of the church is to make disciples of all nations and people groups and bring them all to maturity; the church must then develop leaders from these mature disciples (Forman, Jones, and Miller 54). Existing leaders must discern in whom within their sphere of influence to invest and seek intentionally to develop as leaders.

Leadership development theory includes reflection upon the task of selecting and recruiting emerging leaders. Within the church, leadership development begins and ends with God and what he ordains. God is the one who calls and equips individuals for spiritual leadership. The church must not overlook the role of God working through the Holy Spirit in the process of leadership development:

> The Holy Spirit's initializing and integrating role is a crucial part of every stage of the leadership development process—selection, equipping, maturing, transitions, working through a person to equip others, bringing first a sense of destiny and then a sense of fulfillment as one's giftedness and role converge. He works in the context and the people in that context, through the already existing leaders and in the emerging leader to facilitate, motivate, correct and to enable the new leader to grow and reproduce. The Holy Spirit fills the most crucial role throughout the whole process. (Elliston 99)

The role of the Holy Spirit distinguishes leadership in general from spiritual leadership in the Christian church. Blackaby and Blackaby explain, "Without the Spirit's presence, people may be leaders, but they are not spiritual leaders" (43). Existing leaders in the church simply cooperate with God and the Holy Spirit in the fulfillment of God's purposes.

Scripture does not specifically outline the process of selecting and recruiting leaders. The ministry of Jesus and the early Church described in Acts specifies prayer as the only definitive method for recruitment of leaders (Malphurs and Mancini 129). Character is also a key factor when considering one's potential for leadership. Throughout Scripture, godly character is valued more than the presence of ministry skills. R. Clinton notes, "It is far easier to teach a person ministry skills than it is to change his/her character" (25). Jesus and

Paul selected people of character instead of people of great learning and oratory skill. They modeled what to consider when contemporary leaders search for potential leaders.

When selecting emerging leaders, existing leaders should watch carefully and note how mature disciples respond to God's initiative. Specifically, leaders should recognize how potential leaders respond to integrity checks, obedience checks, word checks, and faith checks in early ministry years and to character process items such as conflict, crisis, isolation, and backlash in the middle ministry years (R. Clinton, 26). An integrity check is a "special kind of process test which God uses to evaluate heart-intent and which God uses as a foundation from which to expand the leader's capacity to influence and/or actually expands that influence" (J. Clinton, "Leadership Development Theory" 103). As events occur in individual lives, emerging leaders have opportunity to choose a response and reveal their character. A challenge calls forth a response and that response results in expansion of influence if the emerging leader successfully passes the challenge (103). McNeal says, "Heart-shaping is an interactive process. Heart-shaping hinges on choices. How the leader responds to God's initiatives codetermines how the story plays out" (*Work of Heart* 188). An emerging leader, therefore, has a great amount of say regarding the pace and direction of his or her development.

Character Formation

Crisis is one method God uses to shape character. Frank Damazio says, "The leader who will benefit the church the most in the long run is the one who has embraced and has been changed by trials, disappointments, sufferings and the mysteries of life" (127). Therefore, when looking for potential leaders, current leadership should look not only for those who are like-minded, cooperative and steady, but also those who have been broken and healed (127-28). These individuals have the potential to continue to grow and influence others through what they have learned. Blackaby and Blackaby believe, "[t]wo factors determine the length of time required for God to develop character worthy of spiritual leadership—trust in God and obedience to God" (54). They contend that in the ordinary experiences and events of life—good, bad, and beyond one's control—instead of in a seminar or course, spiritual leaders emerge (54). Those who persevere through crisis and grow in dependence upon God and faith in God because of failure or hardship become leaders for others to follow.

The local church must be intentional about developing leaders whom God is preparing for leadership responsibilities. For example, a church may take note on how certain individuals serve when deployed into ministry opportunities. Observation of a person's character and competency may indicate whether he or she should be selected for leadership responsibilities (Springle 9). The findings of Albert Appiah's research highlight the need for a deliberate process for the selection and training of leaders in the local church (112). This course of action may involve modeling of behaviors for emerging leaders to incorporate in their own lives. R. Clinton says, "If you decide that you want to use the power of 'modeling' in an intentional way, you can be sure that you will attract a number of emerging leaders" (42). However, nurture may also take place through the intentional teaching of how God grows individuals and by reminding disciples of their true identity (Geiger, Kelley, and Nation 110-11). Although research indicates that an intentional process to select, recruit, and train leaders is vital to the long-term health and effectiveness of the local church, it may be accomplished in a variety of ways (Appiah 54, 112; Beh 45-71, 93).

Training

Once potential leaders are selected and recruited, the leadership development process continues with intentional training and reflection upon process items. Secular organizations and authors understand that experience is a major factor that contributes to an emerging leader's development. Richard L. Hughes, Robert C. Ginnett, and Gordon J. Curphy state that in order to grow, a leader must think about his or her experiences and learn from them (53). They propose an action – observation – reflection model of leadership development, whereby leaders observe the consequences and impact of their actions and reflect upon the appropriateness of original actions (53-54). Joseph A. Raelin agrees. He believes that leadership capacity can arise from life experiences if reflection leads to integration of experiences into one's leadership (61). This theory also finds expression in the medical field where most people are trained through the building blocks of theoretical foundations, integration of theory and practice, mentoring, experience, and specialization (Woodward 205). Skip Bell affirms that emerging leaders learn by doing, which should be followed by reflection with a peer group (104-05). Spiritual leaders understand that these theories correspond to how God developed leaders in the Old Testament and how Jesus and Paul cooperated with God to develop leaders in the New Testament.

This theory of leadership development is beginning to influence how leaders in the church understand the process of lay leadership development. For example, R. Clinton explains Holland's Two Track Analogy, which compares the essential components of leadership development in the church to a train track. The foundation for the track is spiritual formation. The two rails symbolize (1) input/content/information and (2) in-ministry experience or on-the-job training. The ties across the rails refer to dynamic reflection or evaluation and application (62-64). These components may be introduced through several means. The church-based training model outlined by Forman, Jones, and Miller contains three strategic elements: (1) courses that aid in cultivating biblical wisdom, (2) community that facilitates relational learning, and (3) mentoring, which encourages spiritual friendships (62-69). Each of these elements serves to produce leaders with godly wisdom (head), godly character (heart), and skills in ministry and mission (hands). This model is similar to John Eric Adair's three approaches to leadership development: (1) functional—what leaders do, (2) qualities—attributes leaders possess, and (3) knowledge/situational—how much someone knows about the given situation (9-45). Both approaches acknowledge that emerging leaders should seek to build knowledge and skills, but experience and action are vital as well. Malphurs and Mancini identify three training dynamics in their model for lay leadership development in the local church: (1) the core leadership competencies of character, knowledge, skills, and emotions; (2) the learner-driven, content-driven, mentor-driven, and experience-driven means for training; and (3) sixteen venues where training may take place (147). Clearly, leadership development theory may be practiced in a local church in a number of different ways.

Training of leaders will ultimately depend upon one's theoretical foundation for leadership. For example, transactional leadership theory consists of two primary components: (1) contingent reward and (2) management by exception. Contingent reward refers to rewarding followers for satisfactorily completing an assignment. When leaders take corrective measures in response to deviation from expectations or communicated standards, they are managing by exception (Avolio and Bass 3-4). Transformational leadership theory, however, has four components: (1) idealized leadership, when leaders are respected role models, (2) inspirational motivation, where shared vision motivates and inspires, (3) intellectual stimulation, where creativity is encouraged and followers share ideas to address problems, and (4) individualized consideration, where the leader is a coach/mentor that pays attention to the individual needs of the follower (2-3). The goals of transformational leadership are to raise the level of moral maturity of followers, to convert followers into leaders, to broaden and enlarge the interest of followers, to motivate followers to pursue the good of the group over self-interests, and to engage followers in commitment to the effort at hand (1). As might be expected, Bruce J. Avolio and Bernard M. Bass state, "Transformational leadership was higher among those Methodist ministers with greater Sunday church attendance and membership growth ... than among other Methodist ministers" (5). Leaders' views concerning their leadership roles and their followers determine their leader-follower interactions, goals for leadership, and perceptions concerning the significance of leadership development. Although some churches train leaders to accomplish a task, the primary goal of leadership development is the transformation of the leader—the person being trained (Bell 103). Therefore, how a church approaches leadership development reflects how a church understands theology and mission.

Levels of Leadership

An understanding of the different levels of leadership also enables mentors to guide emerging leaders to appropriate leadership contexts. Several levels of leadership exist in the church: self-transcending leadership, supervisory/team leadership, systems/organizational leadership, and strategic leadership (West 3). Adair acknowledges three levels of leadership: team, departmental, and strategic or organizational (46). Additionally, Edgar J. Elliston lists five types of leaders with varied spheres of influence and functions. Type 1 leaders typically lead small groups; type 2 leaders typically lead within a congregation; type 3 leaders are pastors of small congregations; type 4 leaders are pastors of larger churches; and type 5 are administrators in large agencies or organizations (27). These categories are not to be confused with the five levels of leadership James C. Collins presents (20). Collins distinguishes between the leadership qualities and priorities of individuals in leadership roles. Adair, West, and Elliston distinguish among the different contexts, responsibilities, and developmental goals for leaders at the different leadership levels. In the same manner that not every believer will be called to leadership, not every leader is called to attain the same level of leadership.

Leadership development in the local church begins with an understanding of self-leadership. Raelin states, "As an individual, it is important to understand and observe yourself before you can advise others" (65). As emerging leaders become more self-aware, they grow in the area of self-leadership. As individuals grow in the area of self-leadership, they also develop capabilities that facilitate growth toward team leadership (65). This theory corresponds to the premise of Travis Bradberry and Jean Greaves' work:

> We see examples of this every day in our workplaces, our homes, our churches, our schools and our neighborhoods. We observe supposedly brilliant and well-educated people struggle, while others with fewer obvious skills or attributes flourish. And we

ask ourselves why? The answer almost always has to do with this concept called emotional intelligence. (xv)

Self-leadership facilitates leadership beyond the individual as his or her emotional intelligence increases.

The four skills involved with emotional intelligence are self-awareness, self-management, social awareness, and relationship management (Bradberry and Greaves 23-24). Each skill builds upon the one preceding it; therefore, growth in the area of self-management will enable one to understand others better and grow in the area of social awareness. Similar claims were advanced by researchers Alok Baveja and Gayle Porter who considered leadership characteristics that led to creation of growth-oriented workplaces (130). They agree that the place to begin leadership development is in the area of an emerging leader's self-awareness.

Self-awareness involves awareness not only of one's emotions but also of one's relationships, giftedness, calling, character, and life purpose. This awareness may come as an emerging leader reflects upon key questions. According to Bill Hybels, "Is my calling sure?" "Am I developing my gifts?" "Are interior issues undermining my leadership?" and "Is my love for God and people increasing?" comprise a few of such key questions (185-95). Additionally, feedback from coaches or mentors facilitates self-discovery (Raelin 63). They possess different perspectives that may provide valuable input. Another aid for becoming more self-aware is a concept known as double-loop learning, or the willingness to confront one's own views and invite others to do so as well (Hughes, Ginnett, and Curphy 62). Such feedback sheds light upon an emerging leader's personal blind spots.

This reflection and feedback contribute toward a leader's growth in three areas. The first is spiritual formation or character development. The second growth area is ministerial formation, which refers to a leader acquiring ministry skills and knowledge and awareness of spiritual gifts. The third area is strategic formation or knowledge of life purpose and incarnation of ministry philosophy (J. Clinton, "Leadership Development Theory" vi). Each area develops as emerging leaders become more self-aware and learn from actual ministry experiences.

Different levels of leadership require different skills. Although one level is not better than another, in order to serve effectively at higher levels of leadership, certain skills must be mastered. Nick Petrie refers to this concept as vertical development:

In metaphorical terms, horizontal development is like pouring water into an empty glass. The vessel fills up with new content (you learn more leadership techniques). In contrast, vertical development aims to expand the glass itself. Not only does the glass have increased capacity to take in more content, the structure of the vessel itself has been transformed (the manager's mind grows bigger).... Horizontal development can be learned (from an expert), but vertical development must be earned (for yourself).... While personal vertical development impacts individuals, vertical *cultural* development impacts organizations. (original emphasis; 12-15)

Therefore, rather than simply plugging warm bodies into empty positions, the existing leadership in a local church must consider how to raise people to different levels of leadership by focusing upon vertical *cultural* development. Petrie then offers an example: "When a person surfaces the assumptions they have about the way the world works, they get the chance to question those assumptions and allow themselves the opportunity to start to make meaning from a more advanced level" (16). When this critique of mental models becomes a natural part of group discussion, it also becomes part of the church culture.

Range of Lay Leadership Development Strategies in Practice

Lay leadership development strategies in the local church should build upon the foundation of biblical norms and leadership development theory. A strategy implies an intentional plan to carry out certain objectives rather than allowing events to unfold without concern. Although church leaders cannot control all of the elements involved in an individual's leadership development, they should carefully think through the process so that an intentional and effective lay leadership development strategy may take shape. This deliberate outline is necessary because many roads are available to take churches and leaders in any number of different directions.

Mapping

An effective leadership development strategy is dependent upon a well-constructed map. Intentional mapping would aid in marking a church's present location, defining current reality, and setting the course for where the church is going. Certain prerequisites determine whether this mapping process may effectively begin. These conditions include gaining the support of existing leaders, recruiting a leadership development advocate, formation of a leadership development team, agreement on a definition of leadership, and identification of various leadership levels in the church (Malphurs and Mancini 106). Once a pastor or church leader recognizes the need for an intentional strategy for lay leadership development, he or she should select a leader and team in order to create this map. The first step is defining how the church makes disciples. A church should focus its energy on making disciples before focusing on developing leaders because no one can build leaders without first having mature disciples that would be candidates for leadership (191). This process forces the team to define current reality and indicate where they are located on the map designed for lay leadership development.

Perhaps a church is not ready for leadership development. Perhaps the church must focus on evangelism and discipleship in order to move closer toward being ready for a leadership development strategy. In that case, one map could help a church move from its present readiness level to begin effectively making disciples, and another map can take them from discipleship to leadership development. Obviously, one map is not suitable for all occasions.

The next consideration is the available resources. Leadership development in the local church deals primarily with spiritual and human resources. A leadership development team should discern and select emerging leaders growing in spiritual character and demonstrating gifts of leadership by the power of the Holy Spirit (Beh 31). According to Eddie Gibbs, leaders should identify emerging leaders who are pioneers and mission entrepreneurs, not relying solely upon academic elites to become the church leaders that provide ministry to the world (201-02). Jesus chose unlikely people to continue his mission, and church leaders should remember that emerging leaders are not always obvious. Samuel R. Chand provides some questions to consider when recruiting leaders: Can this person do the job? (competence); can this person be trusted? (character); can this individual fit in the church culture? (chemistry); can this emerging leader grow with us? (capacity; 130). These questions and others that are similar can help existing leaders discover candidates for leadership development.

Another consideration is what tools to use to help people grow. Typically, people learn through a variety of means. Teaching, training, educating, instructing, tutoring, coaching, and mentoring are common methods to help people learn (Adair 128-29). Each of these methods works in different situations and contexts. A leadership development team could determine which direction to take, depending on the objectives for each leadership level.

Equipping

Some churches are intentional about equipping lay people and have definite maps or strategies in place to help them achieve their purposes, while other churches' plans are not as explicit. One equipping church in Houston, Texas, simply identifies the right people for leadership and trusts them with leadership responsibilities (Mallory 175). These leaders grow through experience and encouragement. Emerging leaders do not grow in isolation; a trusting, supportive community and network of established leaders are essential. Potential leaders must have proximity and interaction with veteran leaders. Hybels expresses, "How veteran leaders choose to invest in emerging leaders will vary greatly.… But whatever we choose to do, this basic truth stands: Leaders learn best from other leaders" (132-33). Those already in leadership need to make a conscious determination to invest in future leaders.

Leadership development in the local church begins with the existing leader. Unless the lead pastor relinquishes control of the church and entrusts others with leadership, development of leaders cannot materialize. Damazio declares, "Leadership development starts with you the leader using your time to train potential leaders and discern those who can do and those who can lead" (139). He goes on to list eight characteristics of leaders of churches with an emerging-leadership culture: (1) a discerning eye, (2) an effort to reward right character qualities, (3) a shared ministry, (4) no assumptions of people, (5) a development of the total person, (6) an ability to transfer responsibilities, (7) a high retention as a result of valuing people highly, and (8) an intent to lead teams of teams (139-40). Likewise, Adair offers seven key functions of a strategic leader: (1) providing direction, (2) forming strategy and policy, (3) executing, (4) organizing and reorganizing, (5) releasing corporate spirit, (6) connecting to other organizations and society, and (7) choosing leaders and developing future leaders (50). One of the fundamental responsibilities of leaders is to ensure that the baton of leadership transfers successfully to emerging leaders.

One way to facilitate the development of other leaders is for existing leaders to continue their own development. R. Clinton advises, "Our own development will affect not only our own ministries but those leaders who are emerging in our ministries. Quality leaders will emerge best in the context of on-going quality leadership" (402). The Holy Spirit will continue to call leaders in environments where they can grow. By modeling a lifestyle of personal growth, leaders can influence others to grow as well (Petrie 26). Local church leaders should consider their legacy rather than focus upon success, performance, or even strategic plans and doing; legacy results from behavior and relationships with others (Gibbs

215-16). Right behavior and relationships with future leaders will help to create an environment where equipping can take place.

By forming leadership teams, a leader can provide such an environment. Leadership teams allow members to build relationships and sharpen each other (Prov. 27:17). Milfred Minatrea believes in leadership teams:

> Not only do leadership teams strengthen the corporate pursuit of mission, they also effectively develop new leaders. Leadership teams are strengthened as mature and novice leaders contribute alongside one another. The contribution of a variety of people in a leadership team results in a more flexible organization, one that is adept at change. (167)

Leadership teams' members share the responsibilities of leadership and leadership development, keeping existing church leaders from carrying the burden alone. In addition, team building demonstrates trust and respect for the abilities of others, creating growth and development (Appiah 66). Among Adair's seven principles of leadership development is the training of team leaders and providing of opportunities for people to lead. The other five principles are selection of leaders, a plan to have line leaders as mentors, education for leadership, a strategy for leadership development, and a commitment to having the chief executive lead by example from up front (58). Although Adair acknowledges that God grows leaders, he says that organizations could provide opportunities for people to lead (58). The presence and utilization of leadership teams provide one way to offer such leadership opportunities.

Equipping strategies in Scripture provide some guidance for contemporary church leaders. Jesus' plan comprised of spotting potential, carefully selecting in whom to invest, and entrusting disciples with responsibility so that he could coach them to effectiveness (Hybels 126-38). Leadership development norms derived from biblical models are (1) discernment of potential and encouragement to develop it, (2) investment in potential leaders, and (3) responsibility granted to emerging leaders (124). Some authors apply these principles to current church environments and suggest that equipping strategies begin with preparing the soil. This idea means reaching out to people, bringing them into the church, assimilating new believers, and teaching biblical foundations. This process would be followed by connecting people to the church and community and then equipping them through training, affirmation, feedback, evaluation, recognition, reflection, and leader development (Mallory 201). In this sense, equipping is part of the overall strategy of the local church. Grace Church in Orange, California, provides another example of a leadership development strategy in a local church, which they grounded in Scripture. They have created a culture of service by cultivating relationships, helping people discover their gifts, and setting them free to minister with ongoing support and connection with experienced leaders (Sciarra). In each case, the key was training or equipping.

Compared to the amount of literature that deals with leadership development of clergy, few articles and books deal with lay leadership development in the local church. Some principles are easily transferable, yet many churches must learn to adapt principles to their context. Gibbs advises that in order to identify and grow the next generation of leaders, churches should provide training that is accessible and appropriate, joins theory to practice, and is affordable (216). A church's context determines these factors. Churches can also learn how pastors, district superintendents, and other church leaders develop. Studies reveal that emerging leaders benefit the most from having a mentor, on-the-job training, which involves ministry experience followed by reflection and dialogue with a mentor or coach, and formal training in workshops or seminars (Beh 89-91). Most strategies utilize some arrangement of these components.

Before mapping out a lay leadership development strategy, a church should consider the wide range of strategies that exist in practice. Malphurs and Mancini suggest five steps to implementing a lay leadership development strategy: (1) locating emerging leaders, (2) placing leaders in appropriate ministry, (3) providing for development for leaders, (4) evaluating leaders and the leadership development process, and (5) rewarding leaders (127). C. Gene Wilkes also suggests five steps: (1) encouraging potential leaders to serve, (2) qualifying them to serve, (3) understanding their needs, (4) instructing them, and (5) praying for them (189-236). Carson Pue states that Arrow Leadership Ministries operates with a leadership assessment, a leadership development plan, residential seminars, mentoring, leadership clusters, assignments, and structured experiences to develop leaders (17-18). These elements facilitate the progression through five phases of the mentoring matrix at Arrow: (1) discovering self-awareness of abilities, gifts, skills, identity, and weaknesses; (2) letting go of what is holding emerging leaders back and meeting core needs as individuals; (3) visioneering or discovering purpose; (4) implementing the strategy; and (5) sustaining or realizing purpose by maintaining zeal (20-22). These models are only a few of the many strategies of leadership development in practice.

A church's equipping strategy reflects how the church understands humanity's purpose. A believer's developing relationship with God should not be divorced from his or her development as a leader. Hybels points out that one's leadership pathway may correspond to the spiritual pathways. Just as people may grow closer to God through relational, intellectual, service, activist, contemplation, creation, or worship pathways, people may use the same pathway to grow as a leader (215-29). The relationships between emerging leaders and mentors provide one example of applying the relational pathway to leadership development. John C. Maxwell advises leaders to (1) develop personal relationships with people they are equipping, (2) share their dream, (3) ask for commitment, (4) set goals for growth, (5) communicate the fundamentals through training, and (6) give responsibility, authority, and accountability to others (92-110). Training takes place as leaders model, mentor, monitor, motivate, and multiply their leadership (99-101). This strategy is not possible without close relationships between emerging leaders and mentors.

Mentoring

Mentoring, as demonstrated in the ministry of Jesus and the apostle Paul, is a key component of lay leadership development in the local church. According to J. Clinton, "Mentoring is one of the most effective ways of developing emerging leaders" ("Mentoring" 13). Mentoring that aids in lay leadership development is guided by Scripture:

> A mentor in the Biblical sense establishes a close relationship with a protégé and on that basis through fellowship, modeling, advice, encouragement, correction, practical assistance and prayer support influences his understudy to gain a deeper comprehension of divine truth, lead a godlier life and render more effective service to God. (Krallmann 122)

Mentoring is more than a transfer of knowledge; it is a relationship grounded in mission. Jesus called fishermen and tax collectors to observe him, share his life experiences, imitate him, and continue his mission based on what they had learned (44-74). This relationship caused Luke to observe the reaction of the rulers, the elders, and the teachers of the law and record, "When they saw the courage of Peter and John and realized that they were unschooled, ordinary men, they were astonished, and they took note that these men had been with Jesus" (Acts 4:13). Mentoring relationships still have the power to astonish people.

The example of Jesus is an underutilized model for leadership development in the local church. Pat Springle affirms that the content needed by leaders has not changed from past generations, but the method used to communicate that content may need to change to more relational models. He says, "The context for developing leaders is relationships" (7). Relationships were central to the life and ministry of Jesus. Krallmann points out the simplicity of Jesus' mentoring technique. Jesus was relational, informal, oral, and mobile. He was a model, a teacher, an enabler of practical application, an encourager who corrected, and a mentor who emphasized divine empowering (124). These leadership qualities do not require advanced degrees. When describing the mentoring relationships initiated by Jesus, Regi Campbell and Richard Chancy identify eleven methods that Jesus used: (1) purposeful mentor relationships, to fulfill mission, (2) selfless attitude, (3) group context rather than one-on-one, (4) hand-picked protégés, (5) definite period of time, (6) truth of God's Word was at the heart of his teaching, (7) model prayer life, (8) education through practical ministry, (9) utilization of actual life experiences as teaching moments, (10) mutual commitment, and (11) multiplication element (5-7). This technique does not tax a local church budget nor require investigation of curricula; instead, it demands an investment of time and relational capital.

The benefits of mentoring extend beyond the mentor-protégé relationship. Ultimately, mentoring in the pattern of Jesus and Paul expands the kingdom of God:

> With the apostle, as with his Master, all mentoring was mentoring for mission. The paramount goal in raising individuals up to maturity in Christ was not so much their personal spiritual welfare but their being equipped to spread the Gospel message, to multiply a Christlike testimony (cf. 1 Thess 1:6-8). (Krallmann 190)

Mentoring may build up both the mentor and his or her disciple, but the primary purpose is the expansion of the gospel.

By providing accountability, empowerment, and relationship, effective mentoring develops emerging leaders (R. Clinton 67). Unlike classroom instruction through monologues, mentoring provides instruction through modeling, observation, and feedback or input that enhances the process of becoming all that God has called a leader to be (Malphurs and Mancini 155). For the sake of its mission, the church must not overlook the tremendous development potential offered through mentoring:

> We need to expand the craft of equipping from the classroom to the living room, and from the sanctuary to the streets. Equipping needs to move beyond reading

books and writing reports to practicing the craft under the guidance of a mentor. (Woodward 205)

Self-help strategies do not produce effective spiritual leaders; rather, effective leadership development occurs through committed mentoring relationships.

The value of mentoring lies in the flexibility and adaptability inherent in the relationship. Mentoring may occur as a leader identifies emerging leaders, sets an example, teaches, coaches, and releases the protégé (Forman, Jones, and Miller 102-11). Mentoring may take place in a variety of settings and from multiple angles. The constellation model of mentoring advanced by J. Clinton includes upward mentoring (i.e., when a mentor is being mentored by more experienced leaders), downward mentoring, lateral, internal mentoring, and lateral, external mentoring from peers ("Mentoring" 7). Multiple mentor types or roles may combine to provide empowerment in a variety of needed areas. Clinton lists nine mentor types that range from discipler and spiritual guide to sponsor and even historical models (6). A church may also take a team approach to mentoring; a team of leaders can serve as mentors to several emerging leaders simultaneously (Forman, Jones, and Miller 111).

In addition, reverse mentoring is becoming more necessary in the current technology-driven culture. Younger emerging leaders have a great deal to offer existing leaders of traditional churches:

> [T]ransforming wisdom comes to us through surprising, unlikely people if we possess the humility to lay aside our own expertise long enough to embrace the relationship. I cannot call you "mentor" until I have called you "friend...." Flattening the hierarchy that separates two people is the primary contributor to the effectiveness of R[everse]-mentoring because it closes the power distance between them, minimizing the fear of consequences that come with it. (Creps, *Reverse Mentoring* 137, 156)

Reverse mentoring keeps seasoned leaders up to date with the perspectives, motivations, and concerns of the next generation. Leaders may benefit from having a mentor and being a mentor. Discussions may occur around tables or at a bedside in a hospital. At times, the mentor may be younger and less experienced; nonetheless, the reverse mentoring relationship may be the most appropriate for an individual's leadership development.

Lay Leadership Development in Context

Lay leadership development strategies are not transferable from one congregation to another. Each church has a unique context, culture, and community in which lay leadership development strategies must emerge. Theories and practices, norms and principles may inform the shaping process of lay leadership development strategies in a local church, but clones of existing strategies will not produce identical results.

Values Contributing to a Leadership Development Culture

A church's leader determines the church's culture. Church culture starts with an understanding of identity, which emanates from the lead pastor (Nauta 49). Self-identity provides the foundation upon which a culture is created. Sue Mallory states that church culture begins and ends with the senior pastor and that culture determines expectations (56-57). People oftentimes will not rise above expectations, so if churchgoers do not believe God calls them to be more than spectators who attend church in order to have their needs met, they will remain spectators. Self-fulfilling prophecy is the idea that people will rise to the level that is expected from them:

> [P]eople often become what we communicate as our expectations. The structures communicate certain expectations. People may need to resolve the dissonance created between their behavior to adhere to these conditions and their opposing personal beliefs, so beliefs may change over time. (Baveja and Porter 138)

If laypeople are given opportunities to rise above the role of observer and the structure of the church supports leadership development, people are more likely to alter their behavior and become the leaders they were created to be.

The senior pastor's responsibility is to articulate God's expectations for his or her people. This message is necessary in order to prepare the soil for growth:

> Leaders are also responsible for future leadership. They need to identify, develop, and nurture future leaders.... I am talking about how leaders can nurture the roots of an institution, about a sense of continuity, about institutional culture. (DePree 14-15)

While church culture shapes emerging leaders, these emerging leaders can also help to shape the church's culture. This process is a cyclical pattern initiated by the senior leader.

Church culture is a powerful tool for lay leadership development. Each local church has stories, as does each local community. A church's leadership must take time to know and understand the stories of the church and community and communicate culture, using stories (Mallory 61-63). Being mindful of the stories that shaped a church and community equips senior pastors to build fields that become ripe for lay leadership development. Minatrea says, "The missional church is a greenhouse where new leaders are constantly being cultivated" (168). Such a culture describes the *being* of a church. Culture passes through relationships, is understood from the inside, determines the flow of power, and describes what a church *actually* does in practice (Mallory 53-54). Therefore, church culture is a resource that deals with the being and the doing of local church life.

Church values help shape a church's identity. If a church values story, symbol, shared experience, appropriate use of space and Scripture, that church possesses the basic tools to create a suitable leadership development culture (Malphurs and Mancini 217-23). Other values that facilitate growth in believers include a sense of mission, delegated authority, participatory environment, a coaching/encouraging context, space to exercise giftedness, and supportive networks (Elliston 117-37). Instead of guarding individual power, existing leaders need to see emerging leaders the way God sees them. R. Clinton advises existing leaders to trust God—he has been selecting and raising up leaders for a long time (77). A church that values the heart-shaping work of God in individuals will set people free to follow his agenda. This openness to God's leading in turn will shape the church's identity.

Other factors are involved in culture formation as well. Church consultant and author Kennon L. Callahan proclaims, "The best environment for leadership development includes these features: objectives, authority, decision making, continuity, competency, compassion, local development" (152). *Objectives* refers to two to four goals that focus intentionality and direction. This simplicity and focus are preferred to filling a church calendar with activities for the sake of busyness. *Authority* equals power, not responsibilities. When emerging leaders receive authority over a ministry, they possess power to make decisions and take appropriate action. Responsibility without power stunts growth. *Decision making* should be participatory and straightforward rather than a collection of hoops or red tape. *Continuity* refers to long-term objectives and teams that serve together for three years or more. *Competency* means that churches utilize an emerging leader's skills. *Compassion* describes a culture that is patient and kind where coaching takes place. Finally, *local development* means focusing on mission and helping people with their lives and life-purposes (152-71). Together, these values contribute to a leadership development culture.

Authors differ on how to describe the values that contribute to the creation of a leadership development culture; however, many of the concepts they name overlap. For example, Maxwell says the factors that foster growth include a positive attitude by the leader and organization, which corresponds with compassion or supportive networks; consistent accomplishment to build momentum, which corresponds with competency; models of desired leadership, which correspond with a coaching/encouraging context; focus upon potential leader's needs, provision of growth opportunities, which corresponds with local development; and a plan for personal growth (18-32). Likewise, another list of appropriate values includes seeing potential, taking a risk and not expecting excellence, rewarding equippers over doers, giving every leader a baton—a challenge to develop another leader, growing leaders from within the church, and prioritizing lifelong learning (Forman, Jones, and Miller 31-39). Certainly, authors do tend to agree on the beliefs/values that produce environments where leaders are more likely to develop.

These beliefs are similar to those that exist in missional churches. Chand gives seven keys to unleashing a church's potential: (1) control—authority is given to staff/volunteers along with responsibility; (2) basic understanding—leadership grasps the vision, roles, and gifts of the team; (3) leadership—the pastor is committed to the discovery, development of heart and character, and deployment of emerging leaders; (4) element of trust—team members have a mutually trusting relationship; (5) position that is unafraid—team members risk stating opposing views, and are bold and courageous; (6) responsiveness—church takes advantage of open doors; and, (7) execution—decisions are followed by implementation (45-58). Churches with these characteristics are purposeful rather than maintenance oriented. They are moving toward fulfillment of mission, which also means that they are taking risks. By taking risks on unlikely leaders, missional churches move closer toward becoming leadership development churches as well.

Leaders should be intentional with the formation of a church's identity and values. Earl G. Creps illustrates how to begin this process: "Developing an effective RM [reverse mentoring] plan, then, means thinking of it not as the blueprint of a *system* but as the catalyst for a *culture*" (original emphasis; *Reverse Mentoring* 157). Therefore, planning may influence culture. If church leaders are intentional about the values they model, encourage, and reward, they may shape leadership development cultures. Damazio states, "The ways we love, forgive, believe in and handle the failures and flaws of potential leaders all set the culture of leadership" (133). He goes on to list the qualities or values of leadership cultures, which include acceptance, encouragement, affirmation, belief in people, acceptance of risk, inclusiveness, and grace (133). Other authors list similar qualities necessary for leadership development. However, Damazio also says, "A distinguishing mark of great leaders is charisma" (137). I could not find similar statements that referred to leadership traits as sole predictors of effective leadership. Recent studies discount such claims. In fact, expectations of charismatic disposition may actually limit a church's potential to develop leaders.

While some factors facilitate growth, others restrict growth. According to Scott Thumma and Warren Bird, a church's view of membership, use of attendance figures to measure heath and success, views of sanctification, and consumer mentality may contribute to only 20 percent of the church doing 80 percent of the work (66-73). Church leaders must determine whether unspoken standard operating procedures are hindering development of future leaders. Empowerment results from a relationship built upon mutual trust and respect (Long 148-49). When emerging leaders feel restricted from following their passion or God's agenda, something is wrong with the church climate. Jimmy Long observes, "Emerging leaders want the existing leaders to help them find out who they are rather than tell them what to do" (138). Control in the local church should rest in the hands of God rather than in those of a single person or select group of leaders:

> Instead of controlling, we can cultivate and coordinate others to act and lead at all levels of an organization. If we do not empower the emerging leaders of the future, they will walk away from those institutions characterized by a culture of control. (133)

Some churches may have had emerging leaders present but failed to give them space to grow. Vision and purpose provide the boundaries for emerging leaders; within these boundaries, space exists for creativity and innovation (R. Clinton 60). When churches set specific expectations instead of specific boundaries, potential for growth fades.

Control and fear of risk are two of the main culprits that keep churches in maintenance mode. The antidote is grace. Instead of responding to failure with grace, churches typically respond with punishment, which reinforces fear that keeps emerging leaders and churches from taking risks (R. Clinton 58-59). That tendency is why Chand writes, "I encourage pastors to create a culture of experimentation in which creativity is celebrated and failure isn't a tragedy" (116). A culture of grace encourages rather than squelches creativity and development:

> If we are able to create communities that encourage aspiring and existing leaders to gain a deeper understanding of their own God-given uniqueness, and if we are able to create systems of support, we will take a giant leap backward toward the process of leadership outlined in the narrative of Scripture and in the history of our faith. (Bartz 88-89)

Church leaders must provide space for emerging leaders to grow. This space is partly generated by cultures of support, encouragement, and grace.

Behaviors Contributing to a Leadership Development Culture

In addition to certain values that enable leadership development to thrive in a local church a number of actions contribute as well. Being and doing must go together if a church is to represent authentically the body of Christ. Appropriate behavior must support the mission and leadership development values within the church. This activity includes both *what* a local church does and *how* it is done:

> Of all the creators and cultivators who have ever lived, Jesus was the most capable of shaping culture through his own talents and power—and yet the most culture-shaping event of his life is the result of his choice to abandon his talents and power. The resurrection shows us the pattern for culture making in the image of God. Not power, but trust. Not independence, but dependence. (Crouch 145)

Letting go of pride and control helps leaders establish a posture of grace and trust. This position begins with the existing leaders who cultivate leadership development cultures.

Church leaders do not work on a blank canvas. Tradition, Scripture, experience, and reason provide a sketch of what the church should look like. Cultural context provides the unique colors for this sketch. Therefore, every church has something to work with—an existing culture:

> We cannot make culture without culture. And this means that *creation begins with cultivation*—taking care of the good things that culture has already handed on to us. The first responsibility of culture makers is not to make something new but to become fluent in the cultural traditions to which we are responsible.... One who cultivates tries to create the most fertile conditions for good things to survive and thrive. Cultivating also requires weeding—sorting out what does and does not

belong, what will bear fruit and what will choke it out. (original emphasis; Crouch 74-75)

God is active in the world. He was working before current leadership entered the scene and has a mission for the local church. Existing leaders must honor and cultivate God's activity and discern his agenda in a given context before pruning.

Once an appropriate posture is achieved and cultivation of the fruit-bearing elements within the culture has taken place, leaders can take further steps to shape leadership development cultures. Malphurs and Mancini list four actions, which they designate as "brush strokes" for painting new cultures: modeling values, labeling ideas and values, connecting the dots of organizational activity into the big picture, and increasing personal passion (223-33). In a similar fashion, Robert Lewis, Wayne Cordeiro, and Warren Bird advise leaders to huddle and assess the present culture, assess their own role in shaping the future, list values of the preferred culture, enlist buy-in from other leaders, write out and display characteristics of the preferred culture, live and teach these qualities, celebrate and honor those demonstrating these values, and evaluate regularly the church's progress (59-64). The process starts with existing leaders and builds momentum as it spreads through teams to the masses.

Leaders can take certain actions to create a leadership development culture. For example, they should give attention to the organizational structure of the church. Minatrea says, "Cultural engineers help to fashion the structures necessary for the church to serve God's mission effectively" (162). Instead of rejecting all that a church has done and following a personal agenda, the existing leader uses discernment and contextualizes the church's mission (Bartz 89-92). In Minatrea's words, "Cultural engineers do not reject tradition: Rather, they seek to adapt systems and structures for the greatest missional effectiveness in their contexts" (163). Lewis, Cordeiro and Bird give an example of how this process unfolds:

1. Identify and believe God's promises about your church's potential.
2. Model kingdom culture personally.
3. Enlist allies to champion the culture shift.
4. Focus on "what we're becoming."
5. Compare the vision of the future to present reality.
6. Outline a specific, doable pathway.
7. Help it filter through the church and learn from feedback you receive.
8. Stay focused on transformed people, and on those receptive to change.

9. Make heroes of people who best represent the kingdom values.
10. Celebrate every success and give God the glory. (183-84)

Gradually a church can move along the path to a stronger leadership development culture.

Another appropriate characteristic of a leadership development culture is joy. Leaders who empower emerging leaders grant freedom and breathe life into those whom God has called. The result is joy. Max DePree says, "In healthy and rational relationships, rewards complete the process by bringing joy. Joy is an essential ingredient of leadership. Leaders are obligated to provide it" (146). One technique leaders use to provide joy is by receiving input from others, implementing input that is received, and shining the spotlight on others (Long 141). This approach to decision making also keeps control from resting solely upon the lead pastor. It gives room for others to take ownership of the mission of the church and to exercise their gifts. Finally, the act of giving away ministry and joy contributes toward an appropriate evaluation of the current culture. According to DePree, "The signs of outstanding leadership appear primarily among the followers. Are the followers reaching their potential?" (12). A corollary concern would be making sure that people experience joy as they grow in the local church. The level of joy among emerging leaders will reveal the current state of the church's culture.

Measuring Effectiveness of Lay Leadership Development Strategies

Determining which actions to take and in which timing is an art that leaders can learn. The Holy Spirit continues to guide leaders seeking to do the will of God. If leaders prayerfully consider the needs of emerging leaders, the Holy Spirit will help in discerning the proper approach to facilitate an individual's development. Soo Yeong Beh acknowledges, "[F]inding the right balance of training methods for each group of emerging leaders is an art form that varies with different emerging leaders and groups" (111). Some emerging leaders also need to focus on character formation while others may need to focus on ministerial formation or strategic formation and the values that impact ministry philosophy (R. Clinton 72-77). No written formula exists for turning believers into spiritual leaders. Mallory says, "Not only does the local vision of an equipping church undergo continuous revision in practice, but every local example of the equipping church will be unique as well" (170). Forming a leadership development strategy is a work of patience, endurance, and grace.

One vital element in the process of lay leadership development in the local church is intentionality. Leadership development requires deliberate purpose and vision casting. Then deliberate steps help to move closer to that vision. Once the overall vision for leadership development is determined, these steps may include outlining a plan for creating a training environment or culture, building a structure for mentoring relationships, identifying the emerging leaders, and allowing for the grace of God to move in people's lives (R. Clinton 88-89). The guiding forces that influence leadership development each fulfill certain roles. Elliston explains how these elements participate in the growth of emerging leaders:

> Three basic, but very different, critical interactive roles therefore contribute to the intentional development of emerging spiritual leaders: (1) the superintending role of the Holy Spirit, (2) the selecting/equipping role of the existing leaders and church family, and (3) the trusting/obedient role of the emerging leader. (98)

Leaders do not develop without the interdependent relationship of these roles working simultaneously. R. Clinton also emphasizes, "The 'success' of a training program depends on the emerging leader's responses to God. You can create an ideal environment and give the emerging leader every possible benefit but the response to God is still his/hers" (57-58). When the contributing roles are all acknowledged and intentionally brought together, however, masterpieces take shape.

Pastors can become artists who allow unseen potential to become reality. This creative work is accomplished as existing leaders discern God's will; emerging leader's spiritual maturity level, giftedness, calling, commitment; and the ministry context for an appropriate fit (Elliston 111-12). Periodically, existing leaders also must step back and gain a new perspective on current reality. They must evaluate the quality of leaders being formed and the process shaping emerging leaders. That process is as simple and complex as understanding how God develops leaders, identifying those God is in the process of developing, and helping to develop and release those individuals (R. Clinton 4). This scenario is where divine mystery and art come together.

Like great pieces of art, the leadership development strategy of a local church should undergo a form of evaluation. Pastors do not have to become art critics, but they do have a responsibility to keep the church on God's agenda. This accountability requires periodic evaluation. Many people in secular workplaces are familiar with evaluations. Some periodic checks help people grow. Callahan says, "The way people are evaluated shapes who they become" (181). Therefore, the leaders produced by a church reveal the effectiveness of that church's leadership development strategy. J. Clinton gives three factors to consider in the evaluation process: (1) immediate lessons or the ability to identify lessons learned through process items and apply them to future situations, (2) sphere of influence or taking responsibility for and being accountable for one's God-given sphere of influence, and (3) giftedness or the recognition and use of natural abilities, acquired skills, and spiritual gifts in increasingly effective ways (*Leadership Development Theory* 349). Individuals growing in these areas are becoming leaders in the local church.

Evaluations may also take many forms. Informal evaluations, self-evaluations, and formal evaluations are three examples. Informal evaluations are ongoing, routine checks for feedback to make the leadership development strategy as effective as possible. Self-evaluations provide times of reflection for emerging leaders to determine areas of strengths and areas upon which to focus for improvement. Formal evaluations, which may take place each quarter during the initial months of implementing a leadership development strategy, every six months after the strategy has been in place one to two years, then annually, are written forms with questions to determine what is going well, what needs improvement, and what suggestions emerging leaders may contribute (Malphurs and Mancini 184-86). Input from others provides shared responsibility and helps to keep the leadership development strategy in line with the vision and mission of the local church.

Self-evaluation is crucial to keep emerging leaders engaged in the process of his or her own development. In consumer cultures, people expect others to meet their needs. When potential leaders are encouraged to reflect upon how they can meet their own needs, churches cultivate leadership development cultures. Callahan gives seven guidelines to aid with self-evaluation: (1) listing two to four key objectives from the past year, (2) stating results accomplished for each objective, (3) determining personal strengths and weaknesses based upon the results, (4) articulating insights and discoveries made while working on objectives, (5) listing the skills acquired that pertain to the objectives, (6) listing areas where consultation may help with development, and (7) listing two to four more objectives and one to two competencies/skills for the coming year (189-94). This procedure is one way for emerging leaders to monitor progress. The consultive evaluation is another method that builds upon self-evaluation. Leaders share their self-evaluations with a consultive team, find mutual agreement, and form a consensus on objectives for the coming year. The purpose is to provide encouragement and coaching, not correction (195-202). The evaluation process seeks to maximize potential and build leaders up (see Eph. 4:29) for the benefit of emerging leaders who are in the process of becoming who God desires them to be.

When the leadership development strategy of a local church takes shape, it begins to form people. The time spent mapping and training, cultivating and evaluating becomes an investment in kingdom building through the development of leaders. Callahan says, *"The art is to develop persons, not policies"* (original emphasis; 169). A one-size-fits-all method for developing leaders does not exist. Different leaders are ready to receive different strategies (Baveja and Porter 141). Although the work of putting plans into motion may require time and effort as well as careful reasoning and deliberate action, all of these factors will lead toward more mature disciples and better equipped leaders for the local church.

Measuring effectiveness does not mean that a church must keep up with other churches. Context and leadership will dictate which strategies may be most appropriate. Petrie offers a word of caution and hope, which the church may find instructive:

> There are no simple, existing models or programs, which will be sufficient to develop the levels of collective leadership required to meet an increasingly complex future. Instead, an era of rapid innovation will be needed in which organizations experiment with new approaches that combine diverse ideas in new ways and share these with others. (7)

This statement is a word of caution because copying another church will not suffice to accomplish the mission of Jesus. This sentiment is also a word of hope because God will continue to work through innovative leaders who risk going where God is moving. It is okay not to have all of the answers up front. Lay leadership development in the local church involves ambiguity and mystery as well as intentionality, persistence, and hope.

One tool to help pastors in the evaluative process is recent research on training transfer. Studies of best practices in the business world can be used by God to provide an appropriate lens through which existing lay leadership development practices in the church may be examined. One example is a model of transfer offered by Lisa A. Burke and Holly M. Hutchins. This model identifies several factors that contribute to effective transfer of training. In addition to the trainee, supervisors, trainers, peers, and stakeholders either aid or hinder the successful implementation of training in the workplace (Burke and Hutchins, 120). Therefore, learner characteristics, trainer characteristics, design/delivery of the training content, and work environment characteristics all factor into the training transfer process. This information is significant because rather than judging emerging lay leaders alone, an appropriate evaluative process would also consider the many people and elements that influence effective training transfer.

Research on training transfer also may correct misconceptions regarding how lay leadership development effectiveness is measured. Burke and Hutchins state that equipping should not be considered a one-time event that takes place within a classroom. They explained, "Put simply, the transfer problem is not rooted in a specific time phase and thus its remedies should not be either; rather, support for transfer should be an iterative and pervasive process throughout the instructional design process" (121). Evaluation consists of more than checking off on a calendar that specific teaching occurred. Burke and Hutchins reveal what ongoing training may look like in the workplace:

> Training professionals most frequently reported supervisory support (12%) and providing coaching and opportunities to practice new skills and knowledge (11%) as best practices in training transfer. Both areas are consistent with research that explores the role of the work environment in supporting transfer of training … and specifically the role of supervisor support in providing feedback and resources to develop skills.… (116)

Measuring the effectiveness of a church's lay leadership development strategy is clearly a complicated and multifaceted endeavor.

The effectiveness of lay leadership development strategies is difficult to measure, yet it must be measured (Burke and Hutchins 118). Although the literature on leadership development covers different theories, strategies, contextual concerns, and evaluative principles, the current reality in many churches does not reflect a grasp of effective lay leadership development principles. I completed research to discover why leadership development theories are not widely implemented in the day-to-day life of the local church. I measured effectiveness by taking a close look at current reality in a sample of churches of different sizes. This investigation allowed me to determine what churches are doing well in terms of lay leadership development and what needs attention. I also wanted to know who has the best perspective on what is actually taking place. I listened to the perspectives of the pastor and various lay leaders. I wanted to know what is at the heart of why some churches do better at leadership development than others. Therefore, I correlated the stories that unfolded through the data analysis among individuals and among churches. In the end, a new story is being written—the story of greenhouse churches.

Questions for reflection or discussion:

1. What is your role in the development of lay leaders in your local church?
2. How can theology, Scripture, literature on leadership development, or theories inform what happens in your local church regarding lay leadership development?
3. What principles from how people were developed in the Old and New Testaments can you envision occurring in your current context?
4. Have you made maps to get you from point A to point B in your life before? What are the benefits of this practice?
5. What role is mentoring playing in your life right now?
6. How would you describe your local church's culture?
7. How is your church measuring effectiveness in the fulfillment of its mission?
8. How is your church measuring the effectiveness of discipleship and lay leadership development?

Chapter Three
Current Temperature

CHANGE OCCURS when an appropriate response is made in light of current reality. In order to determine what response is the most appropriate in a given situation, a leader must first obtain a proper understanding of factors influencing current reality. Tools such as thermometers help people know what steps to take based on the information these instruments communicate. Before devising plans to increase the production of lay leaders in a local church, pastors and existing church leaders should understand what is going on behind the scenes. They must read the present climate of the church and then take steps toward improving existing conditions.

Secular views concerning leadership and leadership development influence church culture and laity's understanding of church leadership. In representative church governments, church members elect church board members to lead the church. The church board then hires a pastor to serve as the church leader. People in a local church understand leadership as an elected position rather than in terms of a calling. The result of such mental models is that churchgoers are not expected to grow as leaders. Since church members have elected representatives to make decisions and serve in ministry leadership roles, they think they are exempt from doing ministry. Although every person will not be called by God to become a church leader, these misconceptions regarding church leadership prohibit the church from becoming the healthy body of Christ it was meant to be. Pastors are not compelled to invest in potential leaders if they are expected to lead on their own or with other hired staff. Laypeople do not take the risk of leading if they are not elected to recognized leadership roles. Instead of equipping emerging leaders to participate in the mission of God, many local churches settle for maintaining the organization. Such churches look more like businesses instead of missional communities of faith.

Alongside the many maintenance-oriented local churches in America are a number of local churches that refuse to fit into the world's organizational mold. Although the task may be difficult, some pastors do invest in developing emerging leaders who also develop others. I wanted to discover those equipping churches in the Mid-Atlantic District Church of the Nazarene and learn from their methods. The information gained can help to facilitate the development of lay leaders in Christian churches across the country.

In order for plants to grow in a greenhouse, the temperature has to be appropriate. Excessive heat or cold can kill. Stewards of a greenhouse must monitor the temperature to enable the plants to reach their full potential. An instrument to gauge current reality, like a thermometer in the case of an actual greenhouse, is a tool that helps cultivators determine next steps. The data gathered in my study provides a starting point from which leadership development strategies may originate.

A Closer Look at Current Reality

The participants in this study represented eight local churches. These churches are all part of the Mid-Atlantic District Church of the Nazarene but vary in size and location. Two relatively small churches are located in major cities (one in Washington, DC, and one in Baltimore, Maryland). Two large churches are from suburban areas in Maryland. Two mid-sized churches are situated in small cities (one in Delaware and one in Maryland). One small congregation is in rural Pennsylvania, and another is in a small city outside Washington, DC. The pastors in each of these churches completed an open-ended survey (E-mail Interview of Pastors or EIP), and five lay leaders in each church completed a Leadership Development Audit (LDA) except Church G, which only returned four completed LDAs. Copies of each instrument are found in the Appendix.

The pastors in the sample had varying educational levels, ages, and experience. Table 3.1 displays the demographic information obtained from the eight pastors in the sample.

Table 3.1. Demographic Information from Pastors in Sample

Pastor	Age	Years in pastoral ministry	Years at present church	Number of churches served as lead pastor	Number of churches served as staff pastor	Educational level
A	48	20	7	4	0	Master's degree
B	58	32	19	5	1	Doctorate
C	58	25	12	3	1	Doctorate
D	48	23	14	1	1	Master's degree
E	59	32	9	5	0	Master's degree
F	60	37	27	3	1	High School
G	47	13	5	2	2	College
H	60	33	12	3	5	Doctorate

Each pastor has served in pastoral ministry at least thirteen years and within the present local church at least five years. Six of the eight pastors have served in at least three different churches as lead pastor. Six pastors have also served at least one church as a staff pastor. Educational levels vary from high school to college, master's degree, and doctorate.

Five lay leaders were selected by each pastor to complete the LDA. Table 3.2 indicates the age of each lay leader that participated and the number of years that each lay leader has attended the current church. The average age of all thirty-seven lay leader participants who disclosed the information was 46.5 years. The average age of the eight pastors was 54.8 years. Twelve lay leaders (30.8 percent) have attended their present church for less than five years.

Table 3.2. Lay Leaders' Ages and Years in Present Church from Sample

Participant	Age	Years	Participant	Age	Years
Church A			Church E		
A-1	29	0.5	E-1	51	5.0
A-2	37	7.0	E-2	24	15.0
A-3	46	7.0	E-3	52	1.0
A-4	27	4.5	E-4	38	7.0
A-5	28	1.5	E-5	32	0.5
Avg	**33.4**	**4.1**	Avg	39.4	5.7
Church B			Church F		
B-1	71	3.0	F-1	64	17.0
B-2	47	18.0	F-2	41	5.0
B-3	40	19.0	F-3	33	33.0
B-4	45	20.0	F-4	26	4.0
B-5	45	20.0	F-5	31	4.0
Avg	49.6	16.0	Avg	39	12.6
Church C			Church G		
C-1	44	14.0	G-1	49	2.0
C-2	52	11.0	G-2	35	5.0
C-3	dna	dna	G-3	66	5.0
C-4	30	6.0	G-4	70	5.0
C-5	75	0.5	G-5	none	none
Avg	50.3	7.9	Avg	55	4.3

Church D			Church H		
D-1	49	37.0	H-1	62	2.5
D-2	47	3.5	H-2	66	5.0
D-3	dna	18.0	H-3	43	43.0
D-4	73	60.0	H-4	46	28.0
D-5	48	14.0	H-5	58	25.0
Avg	43.4	26.5	Avg	55	20.7

Research Question #1

Before suggesting a prescription for the state of lay leadership development strategies in local churches, I first had to determine current reality. I needed to gain an understanding of what is actually being done in local churches in terms of lay leadership development. My first research question was, "What were pastors of the Mid-Atlantic District Church of the Nazarene doing in regards to leadership development strategies in the local churches?"

The presence of a lay leadership development strategy within a local church is difficult to determine by an outside observer. I met with the district's Missional Ministries Coordinator, Rev. Ken Balch, to discuss which churches should be selected for this study based upon the size of the average weekly worship attendance and whether we thought the church currently possessed an intentional lay leadership development strategy or not. In a few cases, we were wrong. For example, in Table 3.3 two churches that we thought lacked a lay leadership development strategy actually did possess one, according to the pastors in those churches. One church that we thought did have an intentional lay leadership development strategy actually did not.

Table 3.3 reveals why I needed to hear from pastors themselves regarding their lay leadership development attitudes and practices. A solution separated from a clear understanding of the current situation is not a solution at all. The responses to the e-mail interview of pastors painted a picture of what was going on in each local church in terms of lay leadership development. The churches in the sample varied widely in their approaches. One church did not have a specific lay leadership development strategy because it focused upon mission instead. Another pastor assumed lay leadership development happened on its own through the regular life of the church. The third church without an intentional lay leadership development strategy identified a lack of staff, finances, and potential candidates as the primary reasons why a lay leadership development strategy did not exist.

Church	Category (based upon average size of weekly worship attendance)	Perceived to possess an intentional lay leadership development strategy?	Actually possesses an intentional lay leadership development strategy?
A	1	Yes	No
B	1	Yes	Yes
C	1	No	No
D	1	No	No
E	2	Yes	Yes
F	2	No	Yes
G	3	Yes	Yes
H	3	No	Yes

Table 3.3. Perceived and Actual Presence of Lay Leadership Development Strategy

The Greenhouse Church

All eight pastors agreed that lay leadership development was critical to the mission of the local church. What separated those churches that were intentionally developing leaders and those that were not was whether they were able to overcome the obstacles that stood in their way. Obstacles identified by those without an intentional lay leadership development strategy were busyness, lack of resources, and a flawed understanding of leadership in the church. Obstacles identified by those with an intentional lay leadership development strategy were small church mentality, identifying the right candidates, generational expectations, resistance to change, patience with the process, and control. Figure 3.1 gives an example of how pastors responded to the question concerning obstacles.

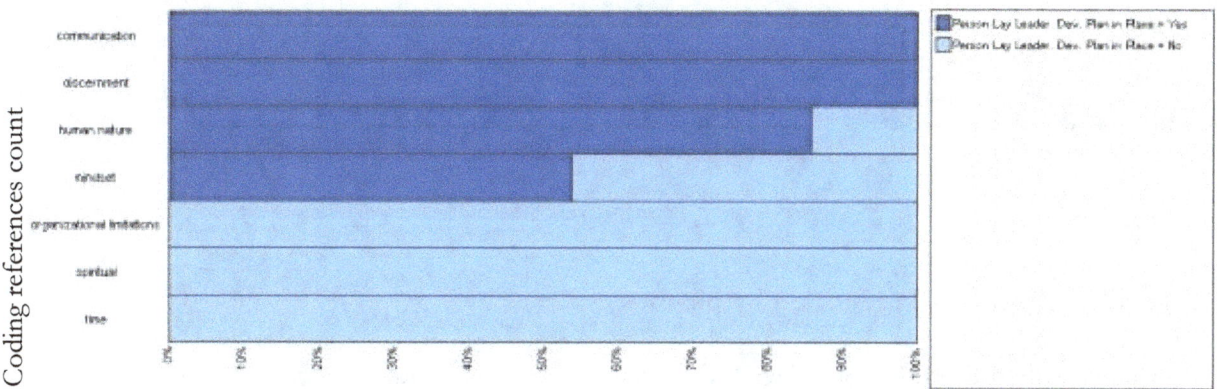

Figure 3.1. Obstacles to formation of lay leadership development strategy.

Those pastors with an intentional lay leadership development plan in place and those without such a plan perceive obstacles differently. For example, only pastors without an intentional lay leadership plan in place mentioned *organizational limitations*, *spiritual* obstacles, and *time*. Dominant obstacles for pastors with an intentional lay leadership plan in place were *communication* about what church leadership means and *discernment* of appropriate candidates for lay leadership development. The majority of references to *human nature* and *mind-set* as obstacles were also made by pastors who found a way to overcome them.

A number of different resources also contributed to the formation of lay leadership development strategies in the churches from the sample. Pastors were asked, "What resources have been most useful in the construction of a lay leadership development strategy?" or, for those without an intentional lay leadership plan in place, "What are the top five resources you have used to help you in your leadership role?" Figure 3.2 illustrates how pastors responded to these questions.

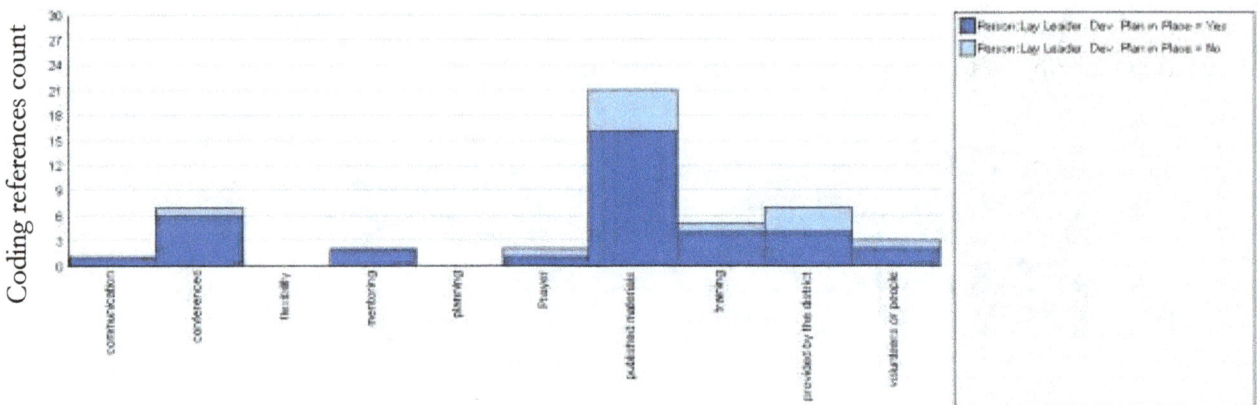

Figure 3.2. Resources identified by pastors.

Pastors who had an intentional lay leadership plan in place and those who did not utilized many of the same resources. *Published resources* were the most frequently referenced by both groups. Other common resources were *conferences*, resources *provided by the district*, *training*, *volunteers*, and *prayer*. *Mentoring* and *communication* were only mentioned as resources by pastors who did have an intentional lay leadership plan in place. (This finding is significant and will be discussed further as something to keep in mind when constructing a lay leadership development strategy for the local church.) References to *flexibility* and *planning* were made by lay leaders but not pastors.

Lay leaders were asked two open-ended questions in order to gain a more complete picture of lay leadership development in the local churches. The first question was, "What would an ideal lay leadership development strategy consist of?" The second open-ended question was, "What suggestions for improvement do you have, if any, for the lay leadership development strategy in your local church?" These responses were also coded as resources for lay leadership development. Figure 3.3 displays the opinions and perspectives of lay leaders concerning what contributes to effective lay leadership development strategies.

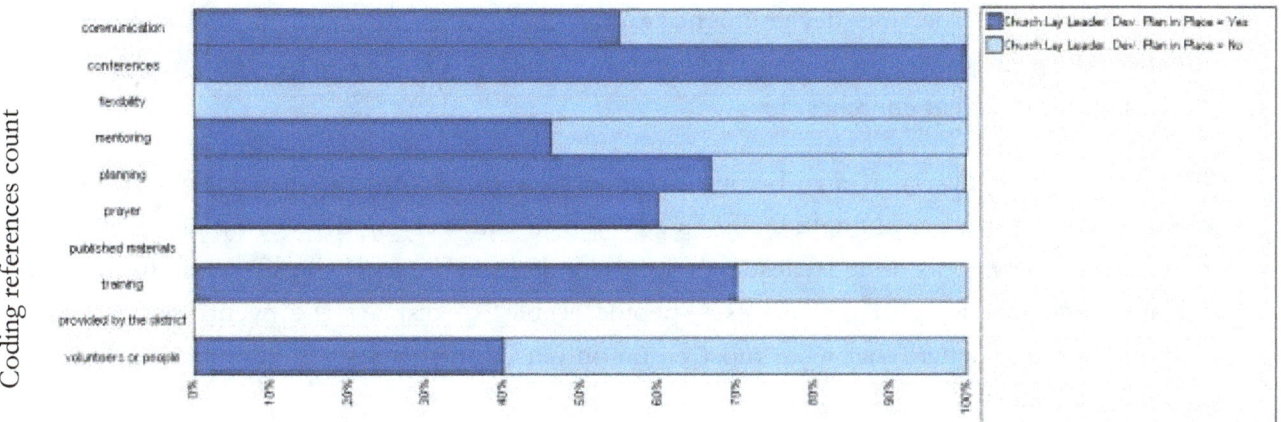

Figure 3.3. Resources identified by lay leaders.

Lay leaders provided a different perspective of leadership development in the local church. None of the twenty-eight lay leaders that answered at least one of the two open-ended questions on the LDA referred to *published resources* or resources *provided by the district*. The pastor may rely upon these resources, but lay leaders are looking elsewhere for their development. Resources such as *communication*, *mentoring*, *planning*, *prayer*, *training*, and *volunteers* were mentioned by lay leaders from churches with an intentional lay leadership development plan in place and from churches without a plan in place. Figure 3.4 shows the different number of churches represented in each of the coding references.

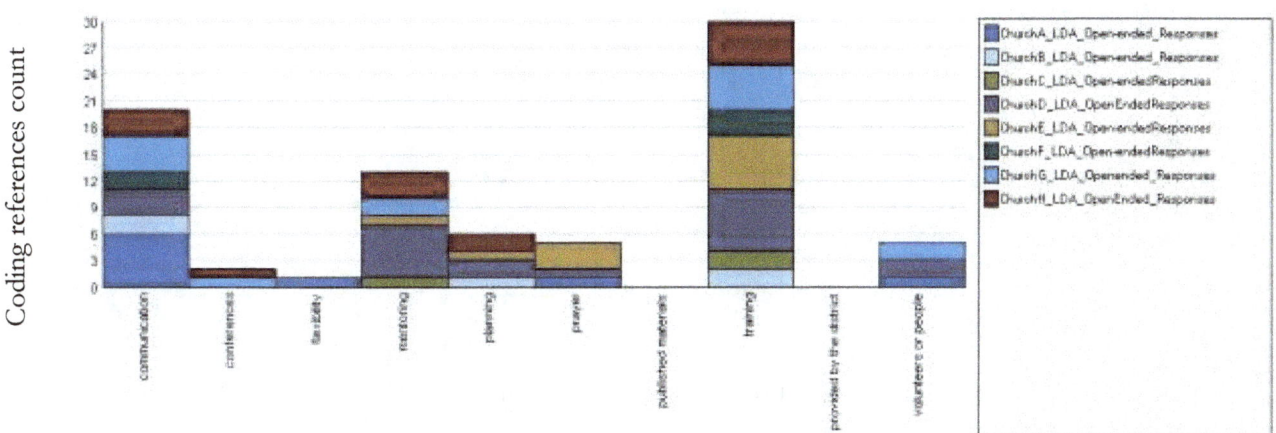

Figure 3.4. Resources identified by churches.

Figure 3.4 reveals what lay leaders are looking for in terms of lay leadership development. Seven of the eight churches in the sample had lay leaders who referred to *training* as a resource for lay leadership development. *Communication* was the next highest reference, mentioned by lay leaders in six different churches, followed by *mentoring*, mentioned by lay leaders in five different churches.

Once again it is clear that an obvious, specific plan to develop lay leaders in different contexts does not exist. Multiple methods are utilized with varying degrees of success. Part of the complexity concerning lay leadership development in the local church stems from the initiators and recipients of the process—people. Table 3.4 displays the twenty-five words with at least four letters that were most commonly used in the pastors' responses to their interview questions.

Table 3.4. EIP Word Frequency

Word	Instances
Church	47
Leadership	37
People	28
Ministry	27
Leaders	21
Group	16

Others	15
Development	12
Help	12
Work	12
Know	11
Community	11
Place	10
Small	10
Think	9
Pastor	9
Give	9
Need	9
Follow	8
Take	8

Personal	8
Process	7
Plan	7
Make	7
Part	7

Other than words such as *church, leadership, ministry, leaders*, and *development*, which were expected due to the subject of the research study, the words that pastors used the most were *people, group*, and *others*. Pastors understand that lay leadership development is primarily about people, groups of people, and others; it is highly personal. The main dilemma pastors face concerning lay leadership development is how to motivate people to become involved in the process.

Five of the eight pastors in the sample indicated that they have an intentional plan to develop people into church leaders. They are making efforts to move potential leaders though a process of development. The strategy, however, looks different in each church. One pastor described the strategy as simply providing opportunities for ministry experiences and training. Another pastor focused upon personal mentorship or investing time and lives into others. One strategy involves helping emerging leaders discover their passion and strengths. Phrases used to describe the shape or structure of the lay leadership development strategies in the different local churches were "top down," "a path to walk" with "relational currents that assist in the flow of development," and "three tiers" consisting of "staff, church board, and ministry champions." Some churches learned from others and used materials such as those from rightnow.org, the K-Church program in the Church of the Nazarene, the REVEAL process made available through Willow Creek Resources, and "other materials that other churches had successfully implemented." The spectrum of lay leadership development strategies in the local churches I studied ranges from the nonexistent to the carefully planned pathway. The churches that are making efforts are using many different resources and approaches.

Research Question #2

After gaining a clearer picture of what churches were doing in terms of lay leadership development, I wanted to evaluate their different strategies. One way to determine the effectiveness of a church's lay leadership development strategy is to evaluate the lay leaders that are being developed in these churches. The second instrument (LDA) was designed to identify the strengths of lay leaders in four characteristics: (1) vision/emergence, (2) church culture, (3) mentoring, and (4) character/inner life. In order to compare the views of pastors to the views of lay leaders within their churches, a revised LDA was also given to the pastors. By comparing the results, I moved closer to answering my second research question: "What were the relationships between a pastor's leadership development strategy and the actual leadership characteristics of church lay leaders in the Mid-Atlantic District Church of the Nazarene?" Through the survey responses, the pastors and lay leaders each told their own version of the same story.

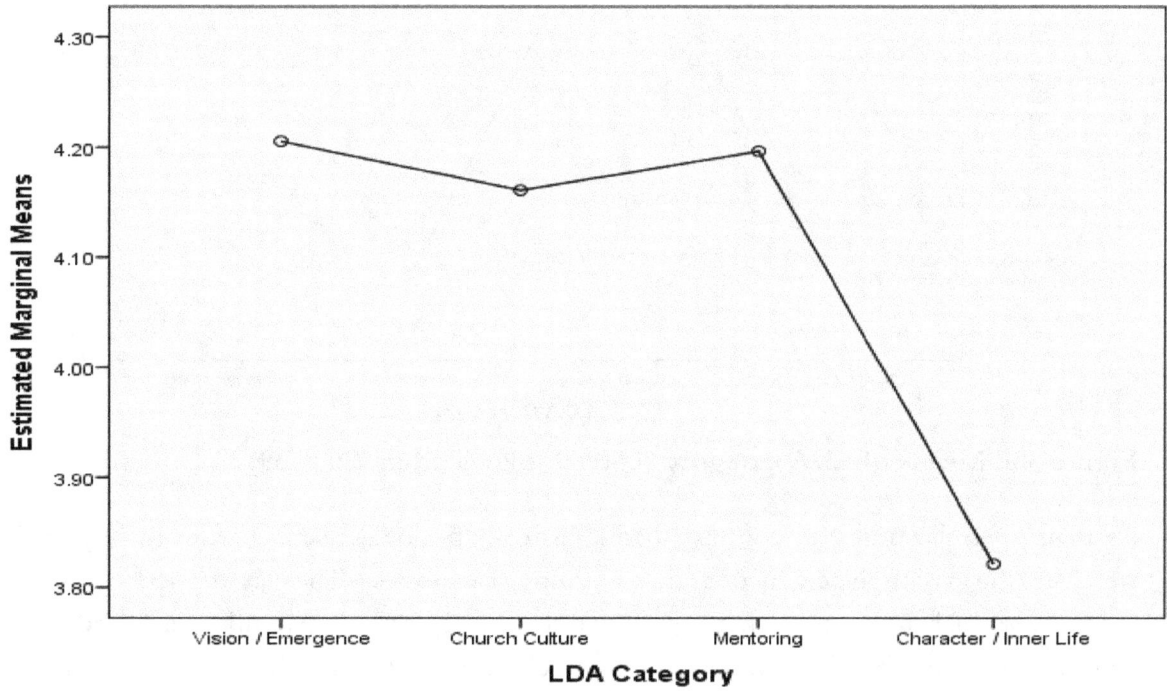

Figure 3.5. Means of LDA category scores for pastors (N = 8).

As Figure 3.5 illustrates, the pastors in the sample believed they were doing well with vision/emergence, mentoring, and creating a culture conducive for lay leadership development. The scores for character/inner life were considerably lower than for the other categories. This finding may indicate that pastors spend the majority of their time and effort forming an environment where individuals can learn and grow, but the inner lives of laypeople is a highly personal matter. Trainers and supervisors can only do so much in the development process; lay leaders also have a responsibility for their own growth and development. This finding may also reflect a need for more attention to the character/inner life of laity. The real reason for the low score is unknown. Further discussion of this topic among pastors would be fascinating and enlightening.

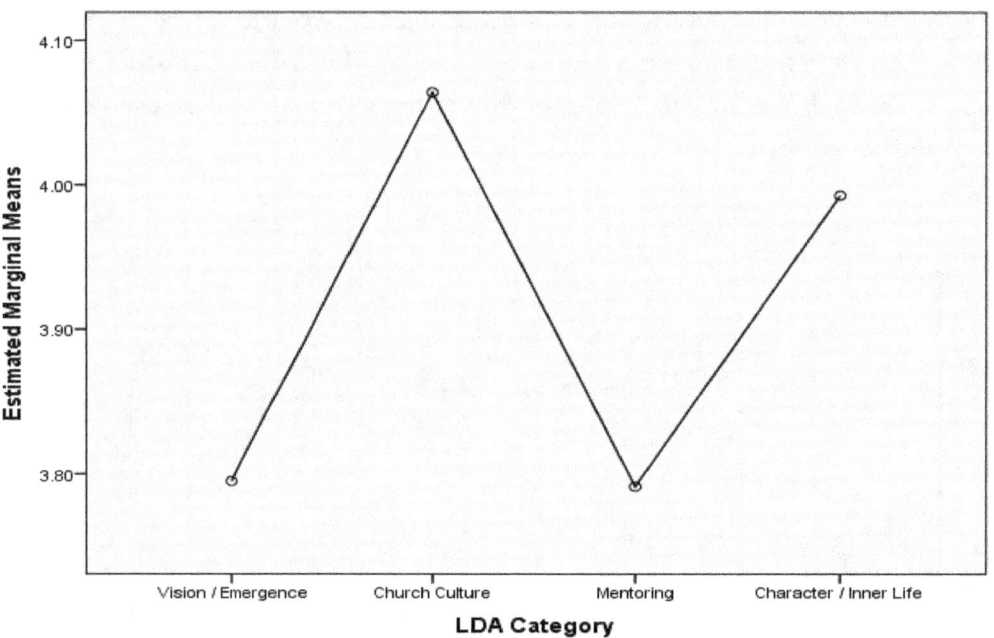

Figure 3.6. Means of LDA category scores for lay leaders (N = 39).

As Figure 3.6 illustrates, in contrast to the pastors, the lowest scores from the lay leaders were in the vision/emergence and mentoring categories. The lay leaders also rated themselves higher in the character/inner life category. Apparently, lay leaders are comfortable with the development of their character, yet they hunger in the areas of vision/emergence and mentoring. While pastors assume they are doing well in these areas, lay leaders yearn for more. They desire to be mentored. Twenty-eight lay leaders answered at

The Greenhouse Church

least one of the two open-ended questions on the LDA. Ten of these individuals (35.7 percent), representing six different churches, used a form of the word *mentor* in their responses. Two of the six churches represented do not currently have a lay leadership development plan in place while four of the six churches do have a lay leadership plan in place. Eight of the twelve references to *mentoring* were in response to the first question ("What would an ideal lay leadership development strategy consist of?"). Four references to *mentoring*, representing four different churches, were in response to the second question ("What suggestions for improvement do you have, if any, for the lay leadership development strategy in your local church?"). Three of the churches represented with a reference to *mentoring* in the second open-ended question on the LDA already have an intentional lay leadership development strategy in place, which indicates that even churches doing something regarding the development of lay leaders could improve in this area. Because half of the churches in the sample had a lay leader who suggested mentoring would improve the church's lay leadership development strategy, I conclude that an improvement in the area of mentoring would greatly help most churches seeking to develop lay leaders. Lay leaders appear to hunger for a shared vision and a mentor. They need to understand where the local church is heading and what their roles as church leaders mean for the future.

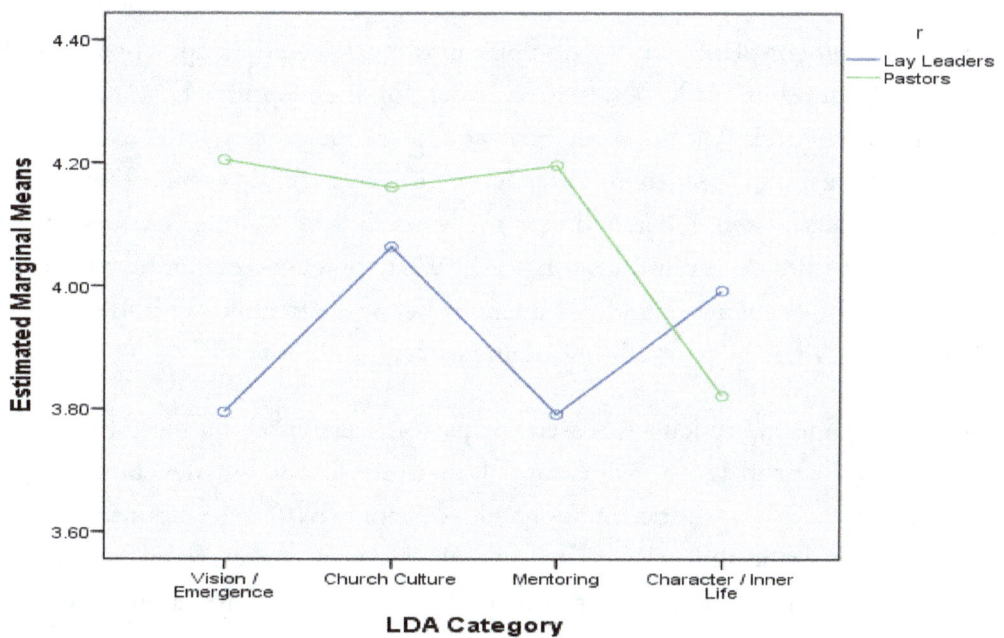

Figure 3.7. Means of LDA category scores for lay leaders (N = 39) and pastors (N = 8).

A combination of the responses from both participant groups appears in Figure 3.7. Research question number two dealt mainly with measuring the effectiveness of lay leadership development strategies led by the pastors in the sample of churches. The findings indicate that pastors think they are doing better with vision/emergence, cultivating a lay leadership development culture, and mentoring than they are at fostering the character/inner life of lay leaders. This statement does not indicate that pastors are not shepherding the characters of their followers, but that character/inner life received lower scores in comparison to the other three categories on the LDA. Lay leaders, however, ranked the areas of vision/emergence and mentoring significantly lower than the areas of church culture and character/inner life. Pastors need to become more aware that emerging leaders desire to share the vision of the pastor and become mentored. Lay leaders generally appear to be satisfied with the church culture and their own character development. Vision/emergence and mentoring are two areas that require more attention.

Research Question #3

A comparison of pastors' lay leadership development strategies and responses from lay leaders led to interesting insights; however, I wanted to know what could be learned from those churches that were doing lay leadership development well. Not every church had a lay leadership development plan to move disciples into church leadership. Those churches that did intentionally develop lay leaders varied widely in their approaches and practices. My purpose for the research was to learn how churches could form effective lay leadership development strategies. I needed to discover churches that were successfully developing emerging lay leaders. Then I could determine workable best practices for lay leadership development. My third research question was, "What practices or contextual factors were most conducive for enabling emerging leaders to become effective lay leaders in their local churches?" Several findings pointed toward an answer.

Four Doctor of Ministry students assessed the pastors' responses on the e-mail interview of pastors in order to provide an evaluation of their lay leadership development strategies. These evaluators used a rubric I designed to score pastors' responses in terms of vision/emergence, leadership development culture, and structure/plan for leadership development. The sum of their scores provided a total score that was used for an overall ranking of leadership development. Across all four categories, those pastors with a leadership development plan in place were rated more highly than those without such a plan.

Churches that were doing something in terms of lay leadership development had a stronger vision, culture, and structure, which made the development of lay leaders more likely. Churches that did not have an intentional plan to develop lay leaders were not as likely to be in a position to develop lay leaders effectively. This finding is not as obvious as it may seem. Many churches do not possess a strategy for lay leadership development because church leaders assume that lay leadership development happens naturally. The churches in my sample differed in the strength of their lay leadership development strategies. Additional data helped to explain what distinguished the stronger churches from the others.

Pastors from eight churches completed the Leadership Development Audit (LDA) to describe their own leadership development plans. Four categories were measured by the LDA—vision/emergence, culture, mentoring, and character. Each category's score is the mean across seven individual items. Mean scores for each category on the LDA by church are shown in Figure 3.8. No one church scored highest or lowest across all categories. Three of Pastor A's category scores—vision/emergence, character, and total—were significantly lower than the mean score. Pastor C's score for culture was significantly higher than the mean score for that category. Otherwise, all pastors' scores fell within the probable range from the category means.

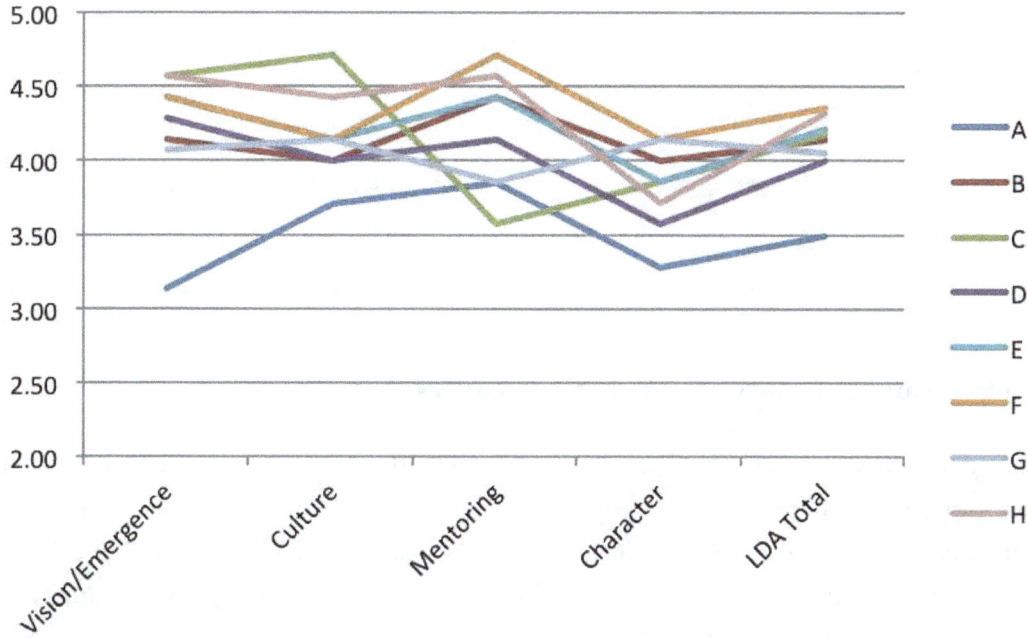

Figure 3.8. Mean LDA scores by church (N =8).

Lay leaders from eight churches also completed the LDA to describe their pastors' leadership development activity. Four categories were measured by the LDA—vision/emergence, culture, mentoring, and character. Each category's score is the mean across seven individual questions on the assessment. Lay leaders' mean scores for each category on the LDA by church are shown in Figure 3.9.

A series of independent samples Mann-Whitney U tests found that lay leaders of individual churches tended to be in agreement with their particular pastors in terms of scores on the LDA categories. This finding adds validity to the scores received from pastors and from lay leaders.

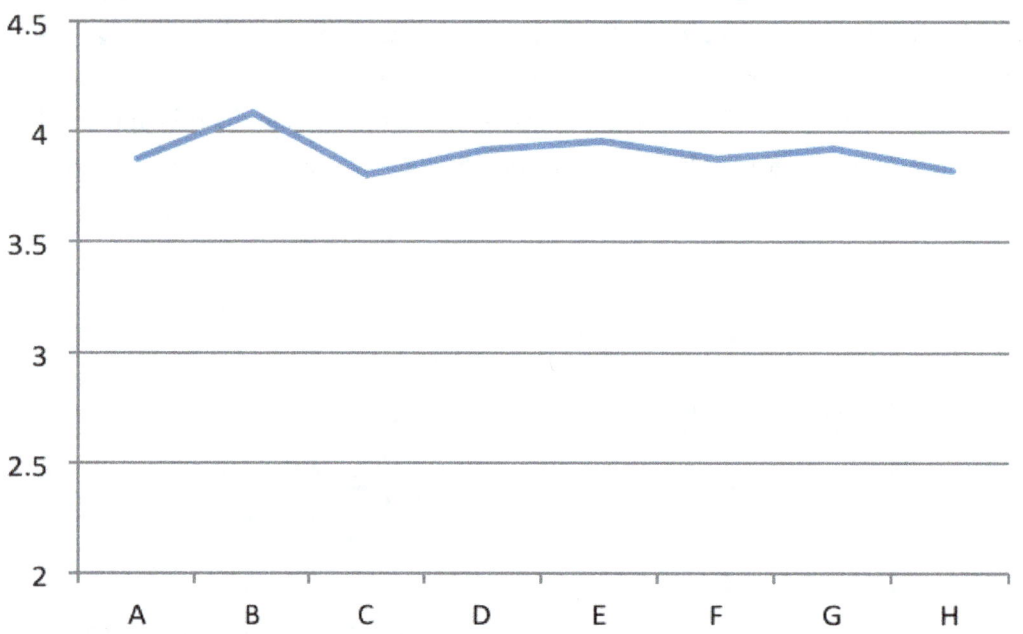

Figure 3.9. Mean LDA scores by church lay leaders (N = 39).

Different groups yielded different opinions concerning the local church with the strongest lay leadership development strategy. Doctor of Ministry students who scored the pastors' EIP responses thought church G was the strongest local church in the sample. Table 3.13 indicates the scores from the Doctor of Ministry student reviewers. According to the pastors' scores on the revised LDA, church F had the highest total scores (see Figure 3.8). According to the lay leaders in the local churches in the sample, church B received the highest total scores (see Figure 3.9). All three churches did have an intentional lay leadership development plan in place.

Table 3.13. Scores from DMin Student Reviewers for EIP Responses

Category	Rv 1	Rv 2	Rv 3	Rv 4	Category	Rv 1	Rv 2	Rv 3	Rv 4
Church A					Church E				
Vision/Emergence	7	5	3	3	Vision/Emergence	8	3	9	7
Culture	6	6	1	7	Culture	9	4	8	7
Structure/Plan	3	2	1	1	Structure/Plan	9	3	9	10
Total	16	13	5	11	Total	26	10	26	24
Church B					Church F				
Vision/Emergence	8	5	9	10	Vision/Emergence	6	3	8	3
Culture	9	7	9	10	Culture	7	3	7	3
Structure/Plan	7	3	7	10	Structure/Plan	7	2	7	7
Total	24	15	25	30	Total	20	8	22	13
Church C					Church G				

Vision/Emergence	3	2	1	3	Vision/Emergence	9	9	10	10
Culture	1	1	1	3	Culture	10	9	10	10
Structure/Plan	2	1	1	1	Structure/Plan	10	9	10	10
Total	6	4	3	7	Total	29	27	30	30
Church D					Church H				
Vision/Emergence	4	3	3	10	Vision/Emergence	9	5	7	10
Culture	2	1	2	7	Culture	9	8	8	10
Structure/Plan	1	1	3	1	Structure/Plan	10	7	7	10
Total	7	7	8	18	Total	28	20	22	30

A comparison of the approaches to lay leadership development in churches G, F, and B led to the discovery of several factors that contribute to effective lay leadership development. Each church represented one of the three categories for the sample, based upon average weekly worship attendance. They represent small, mid-sized, and large churches in the Church of the Nazarene. The one characteristic these churches had in common was that they had an intentional lay leadership development strategy in place. Doing something regarding lay leadership development is better than doing nothing. These churches also offer regular training on spiritual gifts, small group leadership, evangelism, leadership, and ministry. The strategy present in each church is different. One church relies primarily upon personal mentoring. Another church developed a structure that helps move people from spectators to ministers. The third church conveys the idea that all believers are ministers. They may not have as formal a structure in place, but they are intentionally developing leaders by communicating the significance of lay involvement in ministry. This church also provides opportunities for service and relies heavily upon prayer in the process of leadership development. One pastor admitted that the plan is primarily a "one-man band," but he is persistently giving ministry away. The use of REVEAL enabled one church's leadership team to understand the spiritual health of the church. This information was combined with resources from other churches and then contextualized by the team to form its current lay leadership development strategy. None of these three churches have a formal evaluation procedure for their lay leadership development plan.

Summary of Major Findings

The findings from this research project may help district leaders, pastors, and lay leaders transform existing approaches to lay leadership development so that more disciples become church leaders. The research revealed what is actually occurring in local churches in terms of lay leadership development, how pastors' perspectives compare to the perspectives of lay leaders, and how some local churches are successfully developing lay leaders. The major findings include the following:

- Local churches vary widely in their approaches and strategies for lay leadership development.

- Pastors with an intentional lay leadership development plan in place have a different perspective concerning obstacles to that plan than those pastors without an intentional lay leadership plan in place.

- Pastors scored the area of character/inner life the lowest, while lay leaders in their churches scored vision/emergence and mentoring significantly lower than other areas of lay leadership development; and,

- A church with an intentional lay leadership development plan in place will more likely develop more lay leaders than a church without such a plan.

A church that desires to develop believers into lay leaders will incorporate these findings into a strategy that is appropriate for its context. The results will facilitate the church continuing the mission of Jesus to the glory of God by the power of the Holy Spirit.

The Greenhouse Church

Question for reflection or discussion:

1. What surprised you about the findings of the study?
2. What resources are used the most to promote spiritual growth in your church?
3. What obstacles most often prevent people from growing into leadership in your local church?
4. Why do you think that pastors scored their influence on people's character/inner life so low?
5. Why do you think that lay leaders scored vision/emergence and mentoring in their local church so much lower than the pastors of those churches?
6. What do you take away from this research?

Chapter Four
Gardening Tips

GARDENERS and pastors alike can learn from others. Experience and research can inform cultivators so that their strategies are more productive and effective. Existing church leaders would be wise to learn from the mistakes and successes of those who have made attempts at lay leadership development in the local church. A handful of gardening tips can provide valuable insight into the process of nurturing.

Local churches need leaders other than the pastors in order to fulfill the mission of God. People who attend church in American culture are more likely to assume the role of spectator than active participant or leader. The problem with the lack of leaders in local churches does not have a simple solution. I examined the current reality in a sample of local churches to ascertain what was at the heart of the dilemma. Then by comparing other perspectives and churches, I am now able to make some recommendations to improve the current situation.

Different Approaches and Strategies to Lay Leadership Development

My assumptions from personal observation were supported in the findings of my research. Prior to the study, I experienced a lack of lay leadership development in each of the churches I have attended and served. I observed that some churches did nothing in terms of lay leadership development and others made efforts, but confusion was prevalent, especially about what approach was most helpful. In one local church where I served as Pastor of Families with Youth and Lay Development, I was asked to survey other churches and people who could help identify the best curriculum to use for lay leadership development. The result was that we began teaching classes on spiritual gifts using the Network curriculum from Willow Creek Resources. The classes were well received and continued long after I moved to a different church assignment; however, the approach fell far short of a comprehensive lay leadership development plan. Although people became more actively involved in ministry, many components necessary to develop lay leaders were still missing. I attempted to develop lay leaders in the other churches where I also served as Pastor to Families with Youth and Lay Development, as solo pastor, or as Christian education pastor but stayed an average of about two years in each of these assignments and failed to see many results from my efforts.

The churches in the sample had relatively long-term pastors yet were just as uncertain about what to do in regards to developing lay leaders. Prior to reading the survey responses, I could not distinguish with any degree of certainty which churches possessed an intentional lay leadership development strategy and which churches did not. A host of methods existed among those churches that were making efforts in the area of lay leadership development.

Literature suggests that lay leadership development methods should be determined by the context of the local church. Churches in different contexts with different lead pastors should differ in their approaches and strategies. Although the lead pastor determines the culture of the church, which shapes its context, the entire lay leadership development program should not rest upon one individual. The formation of a lay leadership development team would allow a church to decide which lay leadership development strategies are most appropriate in a given local church (Malphurs and Mancini 106). Only one local church in the sample used this team approach in order to map out an intentional lay leadership development plan. By utilizing a team in this manner, the pastor shared responsibility and ownership of the strategy. This church was also one of the top three churches identified through the data analysis.

The theological framework through which I studied lay leadership development in the local churches that participated in the project consisted of three pillars: continuing the ministry of Jesus, to the glory of the Father, through the power of the Holy Spirit. Jesus modeled how to invest in the lives of disciples and how to invite them into a shared life. The approach many pastors take to lay leadership development consists of structured class sessions and seminars rather than a shared life. Pastors appear too busy meeting the expectations of their employers to have time for mentoring. The purpose for lay leadership development is not the establishment of a megachurch, but the glory of God. Current church leaders are preoccupied with doing what is necessary to keep business going. Many churches fail to make the changes necessary to alter the expectations of church members and focus upon God's agenda. The Father does not equate success with numbers but with mission. The different approaches to lay leadership development reflect the different degrees to which a local church understands its mission. Furthermore, since the Holy Spirit and Scripture were not mentioned as resources for the development of lay leadership development strategies, either pastors assumed they were already understood to be resources, or pastors were relying more heavily upon published materials than the supernatural resources God provides.

Different approaches to lay leadership development are to be expected, but some churches are doing nothing. Even though pastors unanimously agreed that lay leadership development is imperative for the local church to fulfill its mission, some local churches fail to have an intentional lay leadership development strategy in place. Pastors are confused about what leadership in the church means and what is necessary to recognize and actually develop emerging leaders. Before pastors train or mentor lay leaders, they must be trained and mentored themselves. Pastors must understand how to turn what they know should be happening in terms of lay leadership development into reality. Lay leadership development theory and knowledge from the literature must be transferred to those on the front lines of lay leadership development. Districts and churches must work together to provide mentors and coaches that will help develop church leaders that, in turn, will develop lay leaders in their local churches.

Different Views Concerning Obstacles

Some churches do well focusing on God's mission, making disciples, and developing leaders. Other churches do not do so well. I have attended both healthy churches and unhealthy churches. During my years of pastoral ministry, I have served under strong leaders and senior pastors that lacked the spiritual gift of leadership. The outside observer oftentimes cannot identify what contributes to the strength of one church while another church in the same town struggles to survive. When individuals begin to participate actively in the life of the local church, they gain a sense of the church culture, the leadership, and some of the key factors that determine the health and strength of the church. One of these factors deals with perspective. Some churches focus upon opportunities and potential while other churches focus upon challenges and problems.

The pastors' responses to the e-mail interview indicate that churches without an intentional lay leadership plan in place see organizational limitations and time as obstacles while barriers for pastors who did have a plan in place dealt with people. Communication and discernment hindered implementation of lay leadership development strategies in the churches that succeeded in putting a plan in place. The problems that kept churches without an intentional lay leadership development strategy from putting one in place dealt with external factors such as the size of the facility or parking lot, low finances, limited time, and the power of Satan. Both groups agreed that human nature or people's unwillingness to change and the mind-set of disciples also impeded the formation of lay leadership development strategies. Some individuals and generations have expectations that oppose the emergence of church leaders. Some churches also found a way to overcome these obstacles in order to follow God's agenda.

The literature on lay leadership development suggests that the pastor sets the tone for the church's identity (Nauta 49). The vision of the pastor eventually becomes a shared vision with the people who choose to follow the pastor. Self-fulfilling prophesy implies that the people of the church will become whom their leader sees them to be (Baveja and Porter 138). When emerging leaders are viewed as leaders and given training and opportunities to succeed or fail, they will eventually see themselves as leaders. However, when emerging leaders are seen as church attenders and are given reasons why training and opportunities do not exist, these individuals eventually see themselves as mere consumers.

Jesus looked beyond obstacles to uncover the potential within his disciples. If church leaders are to continue the ministry of Jesus, they must view people with the eyes of Jesus. No rabbi in his right mind would have hand-selected a tax collector or fishermen as disciples in Jesus' day. Tax collectors were viewed as traitors; fishermen were uneducated. However, in the mind of Jesus, these obstacles were not really obstacles at all. When Jesus looked at the men he chose to follow him, he saw who each of them could become. Again, a theological foundation for lay leadership development in the local church requires church leaders to continue the ministry of Jesus for the glory of the Father by the power of the Holy Spirit. The Trinity enables church leaders to look beyond obstacles to see what is possible.

The perspective church leaders possess regarding obstacles determines the church's ability to overcome those obstacles. Time, Satan, and organizational limitations may make the formation of intentional lay leadership development strategies difficult, but they do not make it impossible. These external factors are simply realities that creative thinkers can conquer by God's wisdom and grace. Some churches have found a way to overcome them. Dealing with people and their different expectations also presents challenges. Identifying what hurdles stand between current reality and God's mission for the local church is half the battle. Once pastors and lay leadership development team members understand what may hinder their progress, they can begin to form tactics to conquer them. They also become more aware how to pray and in what areas they must rely upon God to intervene. Obstacles are opportunities to see God at work. In order for churches to implement lay leadership development strategies successfully, obstacles must be seen as barriers to work and pray through instead of as excuses.

Lay Leaders' Hunger for Vision/Emergence and Mentoring

I have observed that unless an individual is elected or hired into a leadership position in the local church, he or she struggles to share the vision of the pastor and church board. I have talked to individuals who think that a strong distinction is established between the church staff/board members and the rest of the church. Even lay leaders in the church oftentimes assume they must support the vision of the pastor or find another local church in which to serve. The representative structure of church government within the Church of the Nazarene and other denominations actually contributes to the problem. A hierarchy of pastor, church board, and laypeople naturally lends itself to a division of roles and responsibilities. Pastors must make intentional efforts to combat this tendency in order to create an environment where all church members and lay leaders possess a shared vision.

Mentoring has also been virtually nonexistent in the churches to which I have belonged. I have had to seek out mentors throughout my pastoral ministry. The number of church services, ministry events, activities, and meetings that typically fill many church calendars also prohibit the development of mentoring relationships. Unless pastors and lay leaders are trained and expected to make time to invest in others, they seldom mentor emerging leaders.

Research suggests that mentoring is one of the best methods for leadership development (J. Clinton, *Mentoring* 13). Relationships provide the context for training and the sharing of vision in equipping churches (Springle 7; Maxwell 99-101). Lay leadership development deals with people, and people grow primarily through relationships and ministry opportunities, not programs or classes (Woodward 205; Malphurs and Mancini 154-56). Research on training transfer suggests that ongoing support from a supervisor contributes to implementation in the workplace of lessons learned through formal training sessions (Burke and Hutchins 116). In the context of the local church, successful training transfer requires an ongoing relationship with a mentor who can help emerging leaders learn how to utilize skills in actual ministry in the local church.

Through the Old and New Testaments, God developed leaders by sharing a vision, helping emerging leaders see what they could become, and providing mentors for them to follow. Moses heard God's heart to set his people free and learned from Jethro essential leadership skills. Moses passed the baton of leadership and all that he had learned to Joshua. Jesus sat in the Temple at twelve years of age and engaged in conversation with teachers (Luke 2:41-46). He also heard from God's heart; he was to set people free. Jesus passed along to his disciples the baton of leadership with the commission to make disciples and to teach them everything that he had commanded (Matt. 28:16-20). Likewise, Paul had a mentor in Barnabas (Acts 9:26-27; 11:25-26) and mentored young Timothy. In 2 Timothy 2:2 he advised his protégé, "And the things you have heard me say in the presence of many witnesses entrust to reliable people who will also be qualified to teach others." Paul also reminded Timothy of his calling. He gave Timothy a vision of who he was becoming (2 Tim. 3:10-4:5). Vision casting and mentoring were integral components of leadership development in Scripture.

Emerging leaders are crying out for a clear vision, for someone to believe in them, and for mentors. Ministry must move away from programing and closer to relationships in order to return to the heart of God. Pastors should meditate upon their role and calling. They must hear from God his vision for the local church. Then pastors must find emerging leaders and mentor them. They should find a mentor themselves and be a mentor for someone else. Church leaders must also recommit themselves to the mission of God, which is about the development of people and not the development of a church building or busy schedule. Meditation, mentoring, and mission are the main mid-course corrections necessary for churches to develop more lay leaders and to turn local churches in America back to the heart of God.

After I completed the research project, I sent nine questions to lay leaders who agreed to participate in further discussion of lay leadership development in the local church. See Appendix D. One question was, "What role has mentoring played in your lay leadership development?" One lay leader responded, "I didn't have anyone that was my mentor…and really haven't been a mentor to anyone." Another individual answered, "Very little. The pastor has shared with me, but I have not had a mentor." Although a few lay leaders pointed to Sunday School Teachers and Pastors whom they identified as mentors, current reality seemed to indicate that mentoring was not as prevalent as it could be. One respondent summarized the common understanding concerning mentoring, from my research and experience saying, "There has not been a structural format for mentoring; however, I have been able to observe the steps seasoned leaders take." The current reality in many local churches lacks intentional mentoring.

Alongside this dominant theme is a sense of internal drive or calling that causes lay leaders to move beyond a status quo existence. Some lay leaders found that prayer was the key that unlocked their growth and development. One lay leader wrote, "Any success I have had is all due to prayers and God's answer to them." Another lay leader identified the desire to learn as motivation to grow saying, "I am always learning more and eager to do so." This individual went on to say, "Much of the growth in my Christian life has been the result of Christ's leading me through the trials and everyday problems of my life." Trials can serve as excellent classrooms. Another lay leader agreed, answering the question, "Based upon your experiences, what has benefited you the most in your development?" by stating, "Accumulation of knowledge in situational periods of crisis." These responses indicate that some leaders emerge in the church regardless of whether an intentional strategy to develop lay leaders actually exists or not. God is active in people's lives whether church leaders cooperate with him or not. This reality not only demonstrates the grace of God but also illustrates how existing leaders can participate in what God is already doing. God is using relationships with him that are properly maintained through prayer, wrestling sessions with him that are disguised as trials, and creative activity with him that is expressed as a desire to learn to move people into leadership. God is in the business of creating and growing. Local churches can either enable or impede the Vision/Emergence process as God acts in people's lives.

Intentional Plans

My experience has revealed that valuable, long-term outcomes do not occur by accident. Whether a person is trying to lose weight, improve communication, develop relationships with others, or grow closer to God, intentional effort is required. Leadership development also requires intentional effort. Churches that intentionally make time for prayer, evangelism, small groups, and worship find that they are able to maintain and grow in these areas. The churches that did not have an intentional lay leadership plan in place were focused upon areas such as children's ministry, biblical teaching, small group ministry, justice, hospitality, evangelism, and discipleship. These areas all deserve time and attention from church leaders. Since many churches pour all of their energy into areas other than lay leadership development and do not focus upon the development of lay leaders, church leaders must be hired from outside the organization.

The literature indicates that intentional lay leadership development starts with the lead pastor. The pastor must take steps to prioritize lay leadership development, discern who are candidates for leadership development, and then train potential leaders (Damazio 139). The pastor also sets an example for others by working towards his or her own development as a leader (R. Clinton 402; Petrie 26). Leaders cannot expect others to grow if they do not grow themselves. Modeling, mentoring, monitoring, motivating, and multiplying are action verbs that require intentional effort from the pastor if any training of leaders is to occur (Maxwell 99-101). Methods for selecting, training, and mentoring emerging leaders based upon context may vary. According to the research, intentional efforts to develop leaders are vital to the long-term health and effectiveness of the local church (Appiah 54, 112; Beh 45-71, 93). The specific practices and strategy are secondary to the intentionality of the lay leadership development plan.

Jesus understood his mission and was intentional about who he selected as disciples, when he would enter a given city, and how he would conduct his ministry. He set an example for church leaders to follow. The three keys to continuing the ministry of Jesus also require intentionality. Meditation means pausing and reflecting upon God's call and agenda. Mentoring is developing intentional relationships to pass along wisdom and leadership skills. Mission is aligning goals and objectives with the mission of God. Meditation, mentoring, and mission cannot be accomplished apart from thoughtful planning and prayer. A pastor cannot expect to meditate, mentor, or participate effectively in mission by simply doing the work he or she is expected to do. Preaching, visitation, counseling, and teaching can happen without participation in meditation, mentoring, or mission. Most church boards pay the pastor to preach, visit, counsel, and teach. Few churches hold their leader accountable to meditation, mentoring, and mission. Jesus, however, lived and served with relatively little attention to the former practices and more intentional focus upon the latter. Jesus' focus upon meditation, mentoring, and mission enabled him to perform the other activities of ministry. Jesus did not preach or teach as an end in itself. Jesus preached and taught because of his mission. In the life and ministry of Jesus, intentionality informed practice.

Intentionality also should inform practice for church leaders in the twenty-first century. Instead of going through the motions and merely fulfilling pastoral duties, leaders should return to the example of Jesus. Instead of holding on to control, leaders need to give ministry away. The methods will be secondary to intentionality. If church leaders would turn their attention to meditation, they would hear from God how to develop leaders. If church leaders would become more intentional about mentoring, they would not have to increase the church budget to become more involved with lay leadership development. If church leaders intentionally participated in the mission of God, they would discover God's plan to develop lay leaders. Lay leadership development is not another activity to add to the church calendar. Lay leadership development is an intentional process of helping disciples of Jesus reach their potential as ministers. The process may involve training and providing ministry opportunities. The process may mainly consist of mentoring relationships. In order for a church to develop lay leaders, it must intentionally take steps to provide training, ministry opportunities, or mentors. A church's lay leadership development strategy will depend upon the resources available and the church's context. The most important factor is that whatever is done regarding lay leadership development is intentionally done.

Action Steps

The findings of this research project can alter how local church leaders view and engage in lay leadership development. Pastors agree that lay leadership development is important and necessary to accomplish the mission of the local church. Pastors are encouraged to consider the wealth of information available in the literature and develop customized plans for lay leadership development—plans that align with the church's context and mission. Since the literature and research reveal that lay leadership development demands effort and intentionality, pastors will have to discard the notion that leaders develop naturally in the life of the church. This change in perspective will begin to prepare the soil where leaders can grow.

A change in perspective may lead to changes in practices. Some churches will only see the obstacles between current reality and where they are called to be, while others will meet the challenges head on. My desire is that the findings from this research project will provide the encouragement and resources needed for more local church leaders to overcome those obstacles and develop a unique map to develop lay leaders. My research has demonstrated that one size does not fit all when strategies to develop leaders are concerned. Churches of all sizes can become greenhouses where emerging leaders are trained and equipped. The findings also uncover the genuine desire lay leaders possess for mentors. Church leaders who take the mission of God seriously and desire to grow more lay leaders will make tremendous strides by devising an intentional plan for lay leadership development and emphasizing the significance of mentoring relationships. When these steps are taken in the majority of churches instead of in the minority, leaders in the church will no longer be among the endangered species.

One of my favorite questions to ask church leaders is, "What would this look like?" For example, many believers profess that God can move mountains, but few ask themselves, "What would it look like if God were to move mountains in my life?" Therefore, I propose that if church leaders were to apply the findings of this research, the following steps would be taken. The list I provide illustrates a local church growing in the area of lay leadership development.

I recommend that the church board or leadership team review obstacles to lay leadership development. This action would be a tremendous first step. A round table discussion that identified perceived obstacles and strategies to overcome them would begin to bring people to a unified position. The opportunity to voice personal opinions concerning the present state of lay leadership development in the church is another benefit of this type of discussion. I also suggest that the church leaders consider how other churches with similar organizational limitations such as finances and size of congregation are overcoming these obstacles to provide lay leadership development in their setting. The main objective would be to take another look at the obstacles preventing lay leadership development from flourishing and to take action to overcome them.

A second action step I recommend is the planning of quarterly town hall meetings so that pastors and lay leaders can communicate the vision of the church. Many laypeople feel confused concerning the direction of the church. Members of the church need an arena for voicing concerns and questions in a healthy manner. An open environment for communication would help transform the pastor's personal vision to a shared vision and facilitate in the formation of a lay leadership development culture. One of the two local churches in this study that scored the highest on the LDA in the vision/emergence category is using this format to communicate vision.

A third action step involves regular training. One lay leader who participated in the study responded to a follow-up question concerning obstacles that must be overcome:

> People want to feel they are needed. It would be wonderful if church leaders could see the potential in the members of the congregation and encourage those members to step up and share their talents by either leading a ministry or being part of one of the existing ministries in the church.

If leaders saw potential in emerging leaders, training might be valued to a greater degree. The same lay leader also responded to a follow-up question aimed at discovering what the lay leader might do to facilitate the development of leaders in their local church:

> I believe this has to be something that is emphasized from the pulpit. We are not called to be pew warmers—we are called to be the hands and feet of Jesus and that's

done through the various ministries of the local church. I think there needs to be a class that is required when someone joins the church—a class that teaches how to identify our God-given talents and gifts and how they can be used to bless others. ...

Churches with stronger lay leadership development cultures provide regular training to help believers discover their strengths, spiritual gifts, ideal area of ministry, and life purpose. This training may occur at a local, district, or regional event. Church leaders must take advantage of the many resources and training events that are available. These training opportunities should be scheduled on the church calendar and built into the overall lay leadership development strategy of the church.

Fourth, I suggest that pastors and church leaders do what they can to encourage mentoring relationships. Each pastor must find a mentor and be a mentor to someone. Each ministry leader must also do the same thing. It needs to be an expectation of church or ministry leaders that they are being mentored by someone and intentionally mentoring someone. Regular checks on this requirement would provide accountability. These relationships require intentionality. Some training or coaching may be necessary to communicate what to look for and how to get started in a mentoring relationship. Stories from mentors and protégés also should be shared and celebrated. Pastors and church leaders should do whatever they can to take advantage of this underutilized resource for lay leadership development. They must take steps to model, promote, and champion mentor relationships.

A fifth step involves intentionality. I cannot overemphasize the importance of being intentional when devising a lay leadership development strategy. Intentionality begins with the pastor. He or she must make lay leadership development a priority and construct plans to make it a reality. This step might look like regular map-making sessions when church and ministry leaders come together to brainstorm and plan for the development of lay leaders. This creative thinking and planning might occur on an annual or semi-annual basis. The tendency is for each ministry of the church to operate in isolation without a clear connection to the overall vision of the church. Regular map-making sessions would combat this tendency by encouraging ministries to work together to accomplish a greater goal.

A sixth step would start by providing workshops or a sermon series on the significance of meditation, mentoring, and mission. Since lay leadership development is a complicated process that involves, among other categories, vision/emergence, church culture, mentoring, and character/inner life, local churches tend to focus on one area and neglect others. This research study failed to identify a local church that was undeniably strong in each of these four areas (see Figure 3.8). Workshops or a sermon series on meditation, mentoring, and mission would communicate vision, help to shape church culture, promote mentoring relationships, and draw attention to believers' inner life. Then church leaders should discuss ways to build meditation, mentoring, and mission into the DNA of the church. Annual assessments should measure how the church is doing in each of these areas.

Finally, I recommend regular evaluation of the church's lay leadership development strategy. The literature suggests that what is measured gets done (Callahan 181; Burke and Hutchins 118). Three churches in the sample indicated that they measured effectiveness by the observed results or by evidence of life change. Two of these churches were in the top three churches based upon scores from the instruments. None of these pastors specified exactly how they conducted their assessments. Their responses indicated that they used an informal process. None of the churches in the sample did any formal evaluation of lay leadership development in the church. Evaluation goes hand in hand with intentionality. Pastors and church leaders should take steps to be intentional about how lay leadership development is evaluated. This discussion among the staff and members of a leadership team would help move the church toward greater effectiveness in developing lay leaders.

Each local church should focus on an area where improvement is needed. The action steps I suggested provide possible places to start strengthening the existing lay leadership development strategy of the church. The pastor and leadership team need to evaluate current reality and take steps, one at a time, in the direction they plan to go. Results may not be evident immediately, but commitment to the journey will eventually produce lay leaders in the church.

Now that you have been equipped with knowledge concerning your role as a leader in the local church and current reality, let's roll up our sleeves and grow great leaders in God's Greenhouse Church! Let's plant some seeds and water where water is needed. Let's prune and cultivate environments where positive change facilitates growth in people.

Imagine what could happen if instead of non-structured mentoring that lay people had to seek out for themselves a strategy for intentional mentoring was implemented. People are hungry for mentors. One lay leader spoke on behalf of many when he responded to the question, "What do you wish your pastor or other church leaders understood concerning your development as a lay leader?" by saying, "Lay leaders need someone to mentor them and show them the ropes." This individual opened his heart and revealed a deep need through his answers to the four questions that followed. When asked, "What has impeded or hindered your development as a leader?" he wrote, "Not having a mentor." When asked, "What obstacles must be overcome for the development of more lay leaders to occur in more local churches?" he suggested, "Finding and developing a good mentor program." The question, "If you could do something about the current church culture and facilitate the development of lay leaders in your local church, what would you do?" drew out another response dealing with mentoring. He answered, "Pair mature Christians with younger, less mature Christians." The fourth question was, "How would you describe the best example of effective lay leadership development that you have experienced?" This same lay leader lamented, "I don't believe I have received any. I've been self-taught." Ouch.

I also lament that a great deal of potential in people remains dormant because mentors have not been present in their lives to bring it into the light of day. The remedy might be to meditate and act upon Jesus words in John 15:16. Jesus said, "You did not choose me, but I chose you and appointed you so that you might go and bear fruit—fruit that will last—and so that whatever you ask in my name the Father will give you." If you are reading these words I want you to realize that you are chosen and appointed to go and bear fruit that will last. If you follow Jesus, then you are his disciple. As Jesus' disciple, you are chosen and appointed for a purpose. Regardless of your spiritual gifts, profession, vocation, strengths, weaknesses, personality, temperament, or gender, you are called to bear fruit—fruit that will last. What is the fruit that will last? It is nothing less than the gospel lived out in people's lives. Jesus called his disciples to remain connected to the vine as branches that allow potential fruit to become actual fruit. It is the development of people through the gospel. And because Jesus does not expect you to do what he has not equipped you to do, the mission comes with a promise: whatever you ask in Jesus' name will be given by our Father. Do you need help discerning the potential in others? Ask the Father. Do you struggle relating to others—others who are different because God made us all so incredibly unique? Ask the Father for help. Do you feel inadequate to mentor another? Ask the Father to enable you to fulfill your calling as a disciple and as a leader. Go and bear fruit that will last!

Questions for reflection and discussion:

1. How would you summarize the lay leadership development strategy in your church?

2. How can different perspectives concerning obstacles influence church leaders' ability to overcome them?
3. Do you agree that many lay leaders hunger to catch the vision of the local church, to grow into their God-given potential, and to be mentored? Why or why not?
4. Why is intentionality significant in terms of lay leadership development?
5. Which action step from this chapter should become a first step toward improving the lay leadership development culture or strategy in your local church?
6. What short-term goal would you like to achieve in terms of lay leadership development in your church?

Chapter Five
Time to Go!

PLANTS were not created for the greenhouse. The purpose of a greenhouse is to provide optimal conditions for the growth of plants so that needs might be satisfied elsewhere. Some plants need protection from cold weather. For such seedlings, the greenhouse provides a place to grow unhindered by the weather outside which, at times, wars against them. Although it is possible to build a greenhouse and keep everything that is nurtured within its confines, it is not benevolent. Greenhouses are places that offer a safe place to begin. God did not create "plants bearing seed according to their kinds and trees bearing fruit with seed in it according to their kinds" to keep all they might produce within a greenhouse (Gen. 1:12). The same is true of humanity. We were created not for the sake of the greenhouse (the church), but for mission in the world.

Our Father in heaven did not adopt Christians in order for them to spend all of their days in the house of God. My children are growing up. Two of them are college-age young adults preparing to leave the nest within a few years. As parents, my wife and I are trying to help them grow and are planning to prepare them for life outside the walls of our home. The Church has people of varying levels of maturity within its family as well. Some are leaders while others are still in infancy. Some are growing and some are ready to practice what they have been taught beyond the stained-glass walls of the church. If we really are called to be the "salt of the earth" and the "light of the world" (Matt. 5:13, 14) then it is time to go! It is time to prepare emerging lay leaders for their mission.

Salt flavors and preserves, but not when it remains inside a saltshaker. Light illuminates and reveals reality, but not when it remains covered. Growing up in the church, I thought that ministry meant becoming a pastor who ministered to people in the church. I now realize that my position as a full-time technology specialist at a public high school allowed me to minister in ways I never could as a full-time pastor. Instead of meeting expectations and attending countless meetings, I was able to coach soccer and baseball in the community. I experienced the joy of serving God outside the church. I now have the freedom to be salt and light as God intended.

The leader in the church who invests in the lives of emerging leaders and equips them to carry the baton on to others must learn to let go. The task of lay leadership development is not complete apart from release and blessing. Lay leaders need to be encouraged to find their life purpose and be given a blessing when they find a place of service in the world. This may mean that people who have been mentored for years will one day take their skills far from their home church. We need to let them go. This may mean that instead of serving as chair of the finance committee, an individual may step down and start to coach a community sports team. We need to let him/her go. While reflecting upon the role of a church leader in the development of others, God revealed to me a three-fold action plan: Go, Get to Know, and Invite.

Go, Get to Know, and Invite

The greenhouse church is a sending church. Rather than simply inviting people to join what is going on in the local church, the greenhouse church takes seriously the first directive of the Great Commission. The people in the greenhouse church go! They go into the world and rub shoulders with people who do not love God.

Many Christians misunderstand what Jesus meant by "go and make disciples of all nations." They assume it refers to sending missionaries to other countries. However, it is not just a message to career missionaries. Although missionaries must go and preach the gospel to people who have not heard the good news, Christians must also go into their offices, workplaces, neighborhoods, schools, and spheres of influence to be salt and light as well. Believers must go next door, down the street, and across town to re-present Jesus where they live. Young people must go into the classroom and onto the athletic field to make disciples too. In reality, Christians in America are living in a mission field. Every day we encounter people that need to hear the good news of the gospel. They need to know the joy of living according to God's wonderful plan for their lives. It is time that believers who have been fed with God's Word, discipled, and developed as leaders go into the world to make a difference.

Many Christians are uncomfortable rubbing shoulders with the "unsaved," fearing their evil ways will rub off on them. However, Jesus is the model for Christ-ones, and He was called a "friend of tax collectors and sinners" (see Matthew 11:19, NIV). In order to get to know people and build relationships that will lead to a presentation of the gospel, we will have to get involved in the life of the community. We will have to take advantage of opportunities during the week to intentionally develop redemptive relationships. We must pray for God to open people's hearts and lead us to people He is already speaking to. We must also freely give love away. We must practice random acts of kindness and sow the seeds of the gospel far and wide.

I cannot tell you what this will look like in your context. One bit of advice I heard from Bill Hybles at a Leadership Summit in 2008 continues to influence how I determine what I should do. During lunch, I listened to a round table discussion as a panel answered certain questions. One question dealt with how leaders should make decisions in alignment with God's will. Bill Hybles said that each leader needs to have a wrestling session with God. He said that no one should delegate that responsibility to another. Each individual should have time in the ring struggling in prayer with God to understand his agenda. Although I do not know what going into your community will necessarily mean for your church, I can also share another wonderful bit of advice. A former professor was asked by my roommate which seminary he should attend after graduation. The response he received was, "Seek God's will, then do what you want." I have applied this advice to countless situations over the years. When I am unsure what steps to take, I seek God's will. I have a one-on-one wrestling match with God. When the answer does not become clear. I take a step towards what I would most like to see happen. Then I go back to God in prayer and continue to seek his guidance. I also know that since my desire is to see God's will accomplished, my desire and God's will overlap a majority of the time. Sometimes God will be glorified whether we focus on feeding the homeless, tutoring children after school, coaching soccer, or visiting residents in a nursing home. Sometimes God gives us the freedom to choose from a variety of good options. God does not play games like hide-and-seek. When his children earnestly seek to follow him, he is fully capable of making his will known. When he does not, God allows us to exercise the brains that he gave us. The key is to first seek his will. Spend time on the wrestling mat through prayer. God will show you what you must do to go into your world in his name.

Going means going outside the walls of the church to influence the world God loves so much; it does not mean going for good. People in the church have hurt many individuals. Some would rather not be associated with one local church because of relational fractures that have taken place. They have not turned their back on God, but they have given up on the church. I have been hurt by people in the church as well. Yet God chose the church to be his body in our world. We must not lose hope in the local church, whether it is a greenhouse church, traditional church, simple church, missional church, or organic church. The Christian church is the hope for our world. Just this past week a relevant quote appeared at the bottom of our district newsletter. A quote from Dr. Bob Broadbooks,

USA/Canada Regional Director for the Church of the Nazarene said, "A church without broken people is a broken church." We need each other to be the body of Christ and function as God intended. Only then will we be healthy and fit to go into a hostile world in the name of Jesus.

Going is the first part of the Great Commission, which must be accompanied by making disciples. Going into the community to be with unchurched people will not accomplish much unless we go with a God-ordained purpose. When we gather at a park or softball field, we should be intentional about getting to know the people we meet. I struggle with this part of the plan because of my severely introverted nature. I am happy sitting at home reading or writing. Yet God is stretching me and calling me to go beyond my comfort zone. Each disciple of Jesus must find a way to get to know people outside the community of faith.

My experience in churches demonstrates that many Christians struggle getting to know people who are not like them. Believers are comfortable going on mission trips and doing projects in communities to meet various needs but find it more difficult to actually get to know the people receiving their ministry. On Christian radio recently, I heard a story about a gentleman who sat at a coffee shop with a sign on the table: "Free coffee to anyone who hears my story." No one took the man up on his offer. He switched the sign to read: "Free coffee to anyone who tells me their story." The man then had a constant stream of people willing to sit with him and tell him their stories. This tale is instructive to the local church today. We need to listen to people and hear their stories. We need to understand their honest questions, doubts, and disappointments with the church. Instead of placing ads in the newspaper inviting people to come to an unfamiliar place to spend time with unfamiliar people, we need to live in the world and engage people where they are. Common sense informs us that people do not care what we have to say until they know that we care. Getting to know people that have a different worldview is uncomfortable and time-consuming; it is also necessary if we are to continue the mission of Jesus. The greenhouse church encourages emerging leaders to model this approach to outreach and evangelism.

I believe the intentional effort to get to know people is the missing link to many churches' outreach efforts. Church leaders have good intentions and desire to communicate the gospel to a lost world. In the minds of people we are trying to reach however, most Christians are trying to sell them something they are not looking for. The sales strategy for Apple, Inc. is to offer people something they did not know that they needed. After they experience the product, they don't know how they ever lived without it. Shouldn't that describe how people come to Christ as well? People are not looking for what they think the local church provides. Many times, crisis and tragedy must precede a heart that opens to receive the gospel. Yet without relationships with individuals who can share the love of Jesus in the midst of pain and suffering, opportunities to find peace and hope are lost. People need to experience grace, mercy, and compassion from Christians before they actively seek the source of such love. After tasting the goodness of God, they don't know how they ever lived without it. Therefore, in order to reach people, we need to sit down with them and hear their stories. We need to go outside the walls of the greenhouse church and get to know people.

The third activity in this plan is inviting. People may be comfortable inviting acquaintances to a birthday party, social event, or church activity, but Christians are called to invite others to something much bigger than a program on a calendar. Making disciples involves going, getting to know pre-disciples, and inviting them into a relationship with Jesus Christ. A lot of Christians stop after inviting someone to a church service or fellowship activity. The outreach strategy in many of the local churches I have attended included planning an event and inviting people to come. The church leaders meant well. They made efforts to include people who were not currently part of their fellowship, but they did not go and get to know them before inviting people. Furthermore, the invitation was to an activity instead of a process or relationship. When we invite people into the Kingdom of God, we are inviting them to encounter Christ and to continue growing with imperfect believers. This type of invitation is not as neat and tidy as inviting someone to a Sunday School picnic, but it is more life-altering. The greenhouse church is in the business of growing people to become all that God intended for them. Therefore, stewards of the greenhouse church put intentional plans in place to invite people into a process of continual growth and development.

The context will determine what this might look like in actual practice. Theories and reflections help to lay a proper foundation, but at some point, decisions must be made and intentional planning must be implemented and evaluated. As a pastor, I am always looking for ways to make what I know should be happening a reality. I want to help you build a greenhouse church and develop spiritual leaders, so here is one model to consider. In addition to the action steps provided in the previous chapter, what follows is meant to give existing church leaders a starting point from which to build their unique greenhouse church.

A Leadership Development Process

I took what I learned in my studies and constructed a simple process for leadership development that may be used in a local church, in a leadership development club, or in a small group gathering at a workplace or community setting. Leaders are encouraged to modify and build upon this basic model in order to reach people outside the walls of the church, build relationships, and invite them into a life-transforming process of growth. The process begins with self-awareness (Figure 5.1).

Figure 5.1. A Basic Lay Leadership Development Process

Self-Awareness

Self-awareness originates with meditation and builds through the discovery of one's talents, strengths, passion, calling, spiritual gifts, and temperaments. Emerging leaders need to develop the art of seeing self and others through the eyes of Jesus. Calvin Miller explains how our self-concept develops:

> We are writing our best self-definitions, one centered prayer at a time. Our hunger for the inmost God thrills us and defines us. Such prayers tell us

> throughout our lives who we are. Such prayers at last leave us undistinguishable from Christ himself. (116)

Time spent with God will provide opportunities to hear and understand who we are. Rather than listening to the voices of our culture, the media, peers, or naysayers, emerging leaders should be taught how to listen to the voice that matters most—the voice of the One who created them. Every other tool for self-awareness is secondary.

The best way to facilitate growth through the process of leadership development is through modeling and mentoring. Leaders must develop the discipline of prayer and meditation upon the Word of God so emerging leaders might learn from their example. Self-awareness can be demonstrated as leaders share how they have grown to see themselves as God sees them. Emerging leaders also must be taught to view self in relationship to Jesus Christ. In John 15 Jesus taught his disciples that he is the vine, and they are the branches. This provides a great place to start processing self-understanding.

God will help emerging leaders understand how he has created them to fulfill his purposes. A calling is an awareness that God has plans for an individual. A general call applies to all disciples of Jesus, such as loving God and one's neighbor, living a holy life, and spreading the good news of the gospel. These expectations come from commandments to all followers of Jesus. People may also receive a specific call from God to meet a certain need or pursue a particular life purpose. As emerging leaders sense God's leading and take steps in a given direction, the pathway becomes clearer. Others may affirm them as they begin to obey their calling. Efforts will produce fruit and bring fulfillment. Circumstances may also provide additional opportunities to move where God is leading. All of these indicators reveal who God has created emerging leaders to become. With experience will come additional affirmation as God continues to shape leaders for his church.

Several assessments are available to provide additional self-awareness. Answering questions concerning passion, spiritual gifts, personality, temperament, emotional intelligence, and strengths can uncover blind spots and shed light upon different areas of a growing leader's identity. Assessments are tools to facilitate self-awareness and help explain a person's God-given shape. By focusing time and energy in the realm of one's passion and strengths, greater fulfillment and success may be achieved.

Understanding your calling or life purpose is a huge step toward self-awareness as well. Through reflection upon the different aspects of a believer's life, specific themes may emerge. For example, if someone has the spiritual gift of teaching, has a passion for teaching, has been affirmed by others that he/she should be teaching, and has received a call from God to teach, then that individual's life purpose probably has something to do with teaching. Over the years, I have learned to appreciate the benefits of understanding my spiritual gifts, passion, strengths, and calling; however, the concept of life purpose helped me to put all of these pieces together in order to visualize the plans God may have for my life. Based upon what I have learned, I have designed a tool to tie several components together and help emerging leaders discover their life purpose. The questions are found in Appendix E. The inventory will help clarify what God is doing and perhaps lead to greater knowledge about who God created you to be.

The ultimate goal in discovering greater self-awareness is to fulfill one's life purpose. Although numerous assessments aid in this process of self-discovery, God has the final word concerning a growing leader's agenda. A rubber band has a natural shape but may be stretched to fulfill a purpose. Likewise, leaders may be called upon to serve in areas beyond their comfort zone in order to bring glory to God. However, when God does not clearly reveal which decision to make, knowledge of how God created his disciple may lead him/her closer to his/her life purpose.

Community-Awareness

Once an emerging leader gains a better understanding of self, he/she is in a position to achieve greater community-awareness. The process of self-discovery also equips people to understand others better. By learning about different personality types, strengths, and temperaments, individuals can perceive different dynamics at work in others. Emerging leaders must be trained to recognize and appreciate people with different strengths and abilities in order to function effectively on a team. The narrow focus upon self prepares individuals to step back and value the larger picture God is painting as unique disciples work together.

Community-awareness includes team building as well. The local church is the body of Christ (1 Cor. 12:27). Each part has a significant role to play in order for the mission of the church to be fulfilled. Part of the leadership development process involves recognition of the contribution each member makes to achieve mutual goals. This also fosters an appreciation of the work that God is doing among the community and helps to keep focus upon God's agenda.

Since God is also at work in people's lives and in the community outside the walls of the church, the greenhouse church also affirms what God is doing "out there" as well. Leaders should learn to recognize where God is moving in the surrounding community and find ways to partner with organizations beyond the church. The discipline of going into the world and getting to know people who do not love God will not only enable emerging leaders to follow the example of Jesus, but it will also create greater community-awareness. This knowledge will help to reveal problems in society that might be met by the local church. This knowledge will provide a posture of openness to be used by God. This knowledge will help the greenhouse church become involved in the world that God loves so much (John 3:16).

Problem Identification

Self-awareness and community-awareness lead to discovery of problems within a community that might be addressed by an emerging leader from a greenhouse church. A leader's passion may provide clues concerning where a leader might focus his/her time and energy. A God-given burden to meet a particular need provides further evidence for potential areas of service. Experience, resources, and opportunities combine to equip emerging leaders to address a recognized problem. Problem identification requires time spent in prayer. Meditation upon God's Word may help leaders wrestle with God and find clarity over which problems to address. Once an emerging leader understands the culture and community, problems will rise to the surface. Since we live in a fallen world, disciples prayerfully looking for problems *will* find them.

Leaders who mentor and develop other leaders need to help them find a right fit. Not every apparent problem can be addressed. Many problems may be beyond the scope of an emerging leader's capability to help solve. When a person's spiritual gifts, passion, strengths, experience, and calling overlap, a sweet spot emerges. This sweet spot may point towards a life purpose. This area of overlap also reveals the arena where the leader might most effectively meet needs. The greenhouse church helps lay leaders find a place of service that matches how God created them.

A significant part of problem identification involves listening. Emerging leaders are taught how to listen to the voice of God. They listen to the inner reactions to injustice, inequality, addiction, deception, poverty, hunger, idolatry, and other manifestations of sin. Opportunities also arise by actively listening to people in the leader's sphere of influence.

On one occasion several years ago, I went along with a pastor on a follow-up visit after Vacation Bible School. We met the grandmother who was raising her grandson and sent him to our church's outreach program. During the conversation, we realized that within the past year, this grandmother's husband and son (the child's father) had passed away. She expressed grief and lamented over all of the things that were now missing in their lives. One particular tradition she mentioned was the hanging of Christmas lights around the house, which the two men usually did together. That was a divine opportunity for ministry! After we left, the pastor and I agreed that we should send people from our church to the house to hang up Christmas lights. After making a public announcement of our plans, we showed up at the grandmother's house the following Saturday. We had so many people show up from the church to express love to this woman and her grandson that we split up into teams. One group hung Christmas lights. Another group cleaned leaves out of her gutters. Another group raked her yard. She was so grateful that she wrote a letter to the local newspaper. She said that if anyone was looking for a church that knew how to love its neighbors, she knew where they should go. What a wonderful day of service we enjoyed together that day! Those who spend time with people in need and carefully listen not only discover opportunities such as this, but they also experience the joy of seeing God work through them.

Solution Implementation

Some problems cannot be addressed in a single day. They require teams of people working together and crafting a long-term strategy. Solution implementation deals with the process of building plans to address a complex problem. For example, the need for more lay leaders in local churches requires a team and a strategy to overcome existing obstacles. In order to address the problem of few lay leaders in a local church, a leader could find a few others that share the concern, have a map-making session, and take steps to implement the strategy. This segment of the leadership development process is about taking action to solve an identified problem.

Mentoring is key to solution implementation. Leaders should find mentors to help find different routes to a certain destination. Mentors can provide wisdom and resources to reveal possibilities that were not previously visible. Mentoring may even influence leaders in the form of books and other published resources. This process of solution searching has the potential to generate tremendous growth in emerging leaders. Once a problem has been recognized and leaders begin to look for possible solutions, they are hungry to learn.

Mentors should provide opportunities to test possible solutions and create space for the emerging leader to exercise his/her strengths and capabilities.

A fresh investigation of obstacles occurs during the process of finding a solution as well. Strategies should take into account the causes of the problem and everything that stands in the way of a solution becoming reality. A team can then develop plans to overcome hurdles and make strides toward a desired outcome.

In the same manner that some problems cannot be addressed in a single day, some problems will never completely disappear. Despite our best efforts, many problems will remain until Jesus comes again. However, we should still do what we can to make life on earth look more like the kingdom of heaven. The Kingdom of God is already and not yet. We are to pray, "your kingdom come," and then do what we can to make such a request actually materialize as an answered prayer. Mentors may help leaders to set reasonable goals and celebrate small victories whenever progress is made.

Mentor Relationship

Once a leader has grown through the process of self-awareness, community-awareness, problem identification, and solution implementation, that leader is equipped to mentor an emerging leader through the process. Living things grow. When living things cease to grow, they begin to die. Spiritual leaders in the church continue to grow as well. When they cease to grow, they begin to die. One way to facilitate continued growth in a leader is for the leader to have a mentor and be a mentor to someone else. Therefore, the process of lay leadership development in the local church does not reach a finish line until the second coming of Jesus. Leaders learn and grow so they can help others learn and grow as mentors.

Mentoring does not happen in a lecture hall as much as in a coffee shop. Mentoring involves a relationship. In baseball, players run the bases alone. In lay leadership development in the greenhouse church, emerging leaders run the bases of the leadership development process alongside a more experienced leader. Mentor and mentee learn from each other and share life together.

Mentoring is the single greatest step a local church can take to improve lay leadership development in the local church. The process begins with meditation and mentoring accelerates the church's ability to continue the mission of Jesus. Mentoring is the bridge between meditation and mission.

The basic process of leadership development is a place to begin. I do not claim to know exactly what must occur in every context. That question must be worked out, much like a seedling pushing through the dirt to grow in the sunlight. See Appendix F for questions to consider when using this model, but also use the model as a springboard in order to develop your own. Growing is a process—a long, messy, complicated process. Even so, it is worth the effort. Our culture needs more leaders growing through this difficult process to ultimately reflect the Son. These leaders need a place to begin; they need a greenhouse church that invests in them. My prayer is that your church will take the journey necessary to become such a church. If you want to grow cucumbers year-round, you could build a greenhouse. However, if you want to develop emerging leaders that reflect the Son of God, build a greenhouse church and provide a safe place for them to grow.

Questions for reflection or discussion:

1. How would an emphasis upon the order of Go, Get the Know, and Invite change your local church's approach to outreach?
2. In what area of your life would you like to achieve greater self-awareness?
3. Who can help you gain greater understanding concerning who God has created you to be?
4. How well do you recognize and appreciate the strengths of others within the greater community?
5. What organizations or networks exist in your community that could develop into partnerships?
6. What problems exist in your context? Which of these problems are you uniquely equipped to address?
7. What team members could you join to create a map for addressing the problem you have identified?
8. Who is currently mentoring you? Who are potential mentors for you?
9. Who could you begin to form a mentoring relationship with to pass along what you have learned?
10. How well is your local church engaging the world beyond its walls?
11. What steps would lead to greater influence in the lives of those living outside the church?

Postscript
Reflection Upon the Study

THE PROCESS of interviewing pastors and surveying lay leaders was instructive. I am confident in the data analysis and the implications of the findings, but I have also learned how to improve future replications of the research. Each project contains limitations, unexpected observations, and recommendations for other researchers. I took another look at the entire process in order to provide some insight on how others might build upon the research in this study.

This research project consisted of a sample of eight churches; therefore, generalizability is limited. The findings may apply to local churches with similar average weekly attendance figures, settings, and representative structures. The average weekly attendance for the churches in the sample ranged from 35 to 391. Urban, suburban, and rural churches were selected for this project. Churches that are part of the Church of the Nazarene will have polities that resemble the sample. The outcomes of this research may also be generalized to churches of other denominations and contexts through inferential reasoning. One consideration regarding generalizability is the culture that dominates church life and the surrounding community. The culture on the Mid-Atlantic East Coast differs considerably from American culture in the South, Midwest, and West Coast and will require contextualization.

Lay leaders who participated in the study scored church culture relatively high. This finding surprised me. I thought the lowest two areas from the LDA would be church culture and mentoring. Instead, the lowest scores were in vision/emergence and mentoring. Perhaps lay leaders have grown accustomed to the culture of the church and struggle looking at the church culture objectively. Vision/emergence is about seeing what could be instead of what already exists. This skill may be more difficult for lay leaders to master than pastors assume it is.

I was also surprised by the tremendous disparity among the scores from the instruments. I assumed that one local church would outshine all of the others in regards to lay leadership development practices. Instead, I discovered that one church may do well with vision/emergence and struggle in the other areas involved in lay leadership development. No single church was rated the highest in each category on the LDA, and different churches were scored the highest by different groups. This finding reveals the complexity of lay leadership development. Every church has room for improvement. Lay leadership development is not a simple task, nor is it easily mastered. The church leaders that persevered despite the obstacles involved are now reaping the benefits of their labors. They have revealed what is possible.

I began this research project to solve a problem. I have witnessed local churches growing stagnant or declining in vitality due to a lack of leadership. Local churches are not businesses with a boss, employees, and customers. The local church is Jesus' hands and feet. I wanted to find out why believers are not growing into leaders in many local churches. I expected that the situation in most of the churches in my sample would be far worse than they actually were.

The problem of not having sufficient leadership in local churches is a real dilemma, but the story is not over. The story includes a message of hope. Although some pastors contribute to the problem by guarding their power, fighting to maintain control, fearing failure, bowing to expectations, or taking the easy path instead of taking risks, they do not speak for everyone. Many pastors understand the significance of lay leadership development in the local church. They see the problem too. Many pastors are also doing what they can to address the problem. I am encouraged by the efforts being made among the pastors in the sample. Each pastor has a story that includes obstacles and resources, frustrations and victories. Many pastors refuse to give up on people. They continue to nurture and teach them. Pastors pray for them as well. One day these stubborn believers may emerge through God's mysterious intervention and be transformed into spiritual leaders in the church. I believe that most pastors join me in holding on to that hope. Scripture and experience testify to such works of grace. The mere possibility of someone moving from the bleachers to the center of the action and then into leadership keeps many pastors going. When I was in college, I discovered that my greatest joy is giving ministry away. It still is. Through this research project, I discovered that I am not alone. Now the way forward is a bit clearer. Now pastors and laypeople must take action. They must build a greenhouse church. The greenhouse church is just the environment that God's people need to grow and become who they were meant to be.

Appendix A
E-MAIL Interview of Pastors (EIP)

Dear Pastor,

The purpose of the e-mail interview is to obtain information that would contribute to the formation of effective lay leadership development strategies in local churches. Your honest input is essential in this process of data collection. Please answer questions as honestly and completely as you can. In order to help participants understand what I mean by certain terms, here are the definitions of terms that I am using in the research project:

Leader: A disciple of Jesus with credibility, capabilities, and a call to influence or move people in a particular context onto God's agenda (Malphurs and Mancini, *Building Leaders* 20; Blackaby and Blackaby, *Spiritual Leadership* 20).

Leadership Development: "The intentional process of helping established and emerging leaders at every level of ministry to assess and develop their Christian character and to acquire, reinforce, and refine their ministry knowledge and skills" (Malphurs and Mancini 23).

Leadership Development Strategy: A plan for helping people attain the level of spiritual leadership to which God has called them.

Thank you so much for your time and participation!

Craig Taylor

Background Questions

Age: _____ Name of current church: _____

Number of years in pastoral ministry: _____ Number of years at present church: _____

Number of churches you have served as lead pastor: _____ as staff pastor: _____

Educational Level:

○ High School

○ College

○ Master's Degree

○ Doctorate

E-Mail Interview Questions:

1. What words would you use to describe yourself as a leader?

2. What is your local church known for in the community?

3. How would you define success in your local church?

4. How would you define effective leadership in the context of a local church?

5. What are your thoughts concerning the significance of lay leadership development in the local church?

6. How would you describe your lay leadership development practices, if any? Can you provide a few examples?

7. How will you determine which five lay leaders in your church should complete the Leadership Development Audit?

8. Does your church have an intentional plan in place for lay leadership development?

If you answered "Yes" to Question #8, please answer questions #9-#14. If you answered "No" to Question #8, please answer questions #15-#20.

Yes, an intentional lay leadership development plan is in place.

9. How would you describe this plan/strategy?

10. What resources have been most useful in the construction of a lay leadership development strategy?

11. How did you go about implementing your lay leadership development plan?

12. How would you describe the structure or shape of the lay leadership development plan in your church?

13. What obstacles have you faced or had to overcome in the process of implementing a lay leadership development strategy in your church?

14. How does your church measure the effectiveness of your lay leadership development plan?

No intentional plan:

15. What are the primary reasons why an intentional plan for lay leadership development is not in place?

16. What are the top five resources you have used to help you in your leadership role?

17. What areas of ministry are you most focused upon in your church (evangelism, spiritual growth, compassionate ministry, etc.)?

18. How would you describe your church's organizational structure?

19. What obstacles have you faced or had to overcome in the process of fulfilling the church's mission?

20. How does your church measure its effectiveness?

The Greenhouse Church

Appendix B
Leadership Development Audit (LDA)

Dear Lay Leader,

The purpose of the Leadership Development Audit is to obtain information that would contribute to the formation of effective lay leadership development strategies in local churches. Your honest input is essential in this process of data collection. Please answer questions as honestly as you can. In order to help participants, understand what I mean by certain terms, here are the definitions of terms that I am using in the research project:

Leader: A disciple of Jesus with credibility, capabilities, and a call to influence or move people in a particular context onto God's agenda (Malphurs and Mancini, *Building Leaders* 20; Blackaby and Blackaby, *Spiritual Leadership* 20).

Leadership Development (or "helping leaders to grow"): "The intentional process of helping established and emerging leaders at every level of ministry to assess and develop their Christian character and to acquire, reinforce, and refine their ministry knowledge and skills" (Malphurs and Mancini 23).

Please do the following with the attached Leadership Development Audit:

1. Answer the twenty-eight statements on the Leadership Development Audit with your response ranging from 1-5.

2. Answer the final four questions according to your thoughts and opinions.

3. Give your honest responses, understanding that all data collected is confidential and no answers are required for any of the questions.

4. Turn in the Leadership Development Audit, making sure that it is legible, to your pastor within two weeks of receiving it, along with a signed copy of your letter of informed consent.

Thank you so much for your time and participation!

Craig Taylor

The Greenhouse Church

Leadership Development Audit (LDA)

Education:

- ○ High School
- ○ College
- ○ Military training
- ○ Master's Degree
- ○ Doctorate

Church Name:

Number of years you have been in this church:_____ Age: _____

Ministries that you lead:

Respond to each statement by circling the appropriate number:

- 1 = strongly disagree
- 2 = disagree
- 3 = neutral
- 4 = agree
- 5 = strongly agree

This inventory is confidential. Please answer as honestly as possible.

1. I strive to motivate others to work together on common goals.	1	2	3	4	5
2. Risk taking is encouraged in our church.	1	2	3	4	5
3. I want others to follow my example.	1	2	3	4	5

4. I enjoy teaching others.   1   2   3   4   5

5. I have a clear vision for our church.   1   2   3   4   5

6. I know my spiritual gifts and am using them
    in ministry.   1   2   3   4   5

7. I have a mentor for my Christian walk.   1   2   3   4   5

8. I am still growing in my Christian walk.   1   2   3   4   5

9. I know my life purpose.   1   2   3   4   5

10. I welcome feedback from others in my church.   1   2   3   4   5

11. I am mentoring someone.   1   2   3   4   5

12. I pray daily in addition to ritual prayers
    before meals or bedtime.   1   2   3   4   5

13. I help others discover their purpose.   1   2   3   4   5

14. Change is embraced in our church.   1   2   3   4   5

15. I seek out relationships with people
    from younger generations.   1   2   3   4   5

16. I can list the areas of my life that might be
    considered as weaknesses.   1   2   3   4   5

17. I understand how I have grown as a leader
    in the last year.   1   2   3   4   5

18. Laypeople are given appropriate authority
    when they lead ministries in our church.   1   2   3   4   5

The Greenhouse Church

19. I consider myself a lifelong learner.	1	2	3	4	5
20. I am a great follower of other people's leadership.	1	2	3	4	5
21. This church has helped me realize how I can influence others as a leader in the church.	1	2	3	4	5
22. Our pastor helps leaders develop their potential.	1	2	3	4	5
23. I have many conversations with the pastor about ministry.	1	2	3	4	5
24. I understand how to compensate for my weaknesses.	1	2	3	4	5
25. I recognize how future leaders become actual leaders in the church.	1	2	3	4	5
26. Our church equips people to serve in ministry.	1	2	3	4	5
27. I feel responsible to help future leaders in the church grow.	1	2	3	4	5
28. I am skilled in conflict resolution.	1	2	3	4	5

29. What would an ideal lay leadership development strategy consist of?

30. What suggestions for improvement do you have, if any, for the lay leadership development strategy in your local church?

31. Do you know anyone else whom I should talk to about his or her thoughts/feelings about lay leadership development in the local church? What is his or her name and church?

Name: _____ Church: _____

32. Would you be willing to participate further in a focus group to discuss lay leadership development in the local church?   Yes   No

If so, please give your preferred means to be contacted (e-mail address or phone number):

Appendix C
Revised LDA For Pastors In Sample

Leadership Development Audit (LDA)

Church Name:

Respond to each statement by circling the appropriate number:

1 = strongly disagree

2 = disagree

3 = neutral

4 = agree

5 = strongly agree

This inventory is confidential. Please answer as honestly as possible.

1. I strive to motivate lay leaders to work together on common goals.	1	2	3	4	5
2. Risk taking is encouraged in our church.	1	2	3	4	5
3. I encourage lay leaders to follow my example.	1	2	3	4	5
4. I enjoy teaching others.	1	2	3	4	5
5. I have a clear vision for our church.	1	2	3	4	5
6. I enable lay leaders to discover their spiritual gifts and use them in ministry.	1	2	3	4	5
7. I have a mentor for my Christian walk.	1	2	3	4	5

8. Our lay leaders know they are expected to continue
    growing in their Christian walk.　　　　　　　　　1　　2　　3　　4　　5

9. I help leaders discover their life purpose.　　　　　　1　　2　　3　　4　　5

10. I welcome feedback in the church.　　　　　　　　　1　　2　　3　　4　　5

11. I set an example by mentoring someone.　　　　　　1　　2　　3　　4　　5

12. I teach people to pray daily in addition
    to ritual prayers before meals or bedtime.　　　　　1　　2　　3　　4　　5

13. I help church leaders help others discover
    their purpose.　　　　　　　　　　　　　　　　　1　　2　　3　　4　　5

14. Change is embraced in our church.　　　　　　　　1　　2　　3　　4　　5

15. I model how to seek out relationships with people
    from younger generations.　　　　　　　　　　　 1　　2　　3　　4　　5

16. I teach how to recognize areas of a lay leader's life
    that might be considered as weaknesses.　　　　　1　　2　　3　　4　　5

17. I help others understand how they have grown
    as leaders in the last year.　　　　　　　　　　　1　　2　　3　　4　　5

18. Laypeople are given appropriate authority
    when they lead ministries in our church.　　　　　1　　2　　3　　4　　5

19. I demonstrate that leaders are lifelong learners.　　　1　　2　　3　　4　　5

20. I teach lay leaders how to become great followers
    of other people's leadership.　　　　　　　　　　1　　2　　3　　4　　5

21. I help lay leaders realize how they can influence
    others as a leader in the church.   1   2   3   4   5

22. I help lay leaders develop their potential.   1   2   3   4   5

23. I have many conversations with lay leaders
    about ministry.   1   2   3   4   5

24. I help lay leaders understand how to compensate
    for their weaknesses.   1   2   3   4   5

25. I recognize how future leaders become actual leaders
    in the church.   1   2   3   4   5

26. Our church equips people to serve in ministry.   1   2   3   4   5

27. I feel responsible to help present leaders assume
    responsibility for the growth of future leaders
    in the church.   1   2   3   4   5

28. I teach lay leaders skills in conflict resolution.   1   2   3   4   5

29. What would an ideal lay leadership development strategy consist of?

30. What improvements, if any, would you like to implement in the lay leadership
    development strategy in your local church?

Appendix D
Additional Follow-up Questions for Lay Leaders

Questions

1. How would you describe your development as a leader in the local church?

2. Based upon your experiences, what has benefited you the most in your development?

3. What role has mentoring played in your lay leadership development?

4. What do you wish your pastor or other church leaders understood concerning your development as a lay leader?

5. What has impeded or hindered your development as a leader?

6. What obstacles must be overcome for the development of more lay leaders to occur in more local churches?

7. If you could do something about the current church culture and facilitate the development of lay leaders in your local church, what would you do?

8. How would you describe the best example of effective lay leadership development that your have experienced?

9. What question didn't I ask that I should have asked?

Appendix E
Questions for Discovering Life Purpose

Needs

1) What do you think are the greatest needs of the community?

2) What burdens do you carry which you feel compelled to address?

3) In what ways can you be a blessing to others?

Experience & Successes

1) What life experiences have prepared you to address the needs mentioned above?

2) In what areas of your life have you experienced results that were most positive?

Confirmation & Counsel

1) What have you done that caused people to take notice and express affirmation?

2) What themes are repeated when people give you advice concerning the direction of your life?

3) What have people told you that you are good at doing?

Gifts & Skills

1) If you have taken a spiritual gifts inventory, what are your spiritual gifts?

2) If you have taken a StrengthsFinders assessment, what are your top five strengths?

3) What are your talents?

4) What are you uniquely gifted to offer in service to others?

Intuition

1) What do you sense in your spirit that you should do with your life?

2) If you were to counsel yourself, what advice would you give?

Passion

1) If you could immediately do anything and be successful, what would you do?

2) What would you like to achieve during your lifetime?

3) What do those who know you best say that you are most passionate about?

4) What cause/problem do you most enjoy talking about?

5) What areas of service bring you the most fulfillment?

Revelation & Calling

1) When God speaks to you concerning your life, what does He say?

2) If you can visualize yourself sitting at the feet of Jesus and He was to look into your eyes and speak to your heart, what would He say?

3) What has God revealed to you about how you should spend the rest of your days?

4) What is God calling you to do with your life?

Life Circumstances

1) How does your present situation in life contribute to your service to God?

2) Why has God created you for such a time as this?

Overlapping Themes

1) Looking back over your written responses, what themes keep repeating?

2) In what areas do you notice overlap?

3) How do the answers to the questions above all come together?

4) How would you answer someone who asked you about your life purpose?

5) Based upon what you are learning about yourself, what is your personal mission statement?

6) What obstacles keep you from moving in the direction of your life purpose?

7) What are the next steps that you need to take to move closer to fulfilling your life purpose?

8) Who can help keep you moving in the direction of your life purpose?

Appendix F
Questions to Consider in the Model for Leadership Development

Questions regarding Self-Awareness:

How does God see me?

What does God want me to do about ___?

What is my purpose?

How do I feel about ___?

Why do I feel ___ about ___?

What am I specially gifted to do? Why?

What are my passions/strengths?

How does ___ affect me?

Questions regarding Community-Awareness:

What organizations are already tackling this issue?

What network can I plug into?

How are most people responding to this issue?

Why would the community care about ___?

How can I motivate the community?

What is the significance of this response?

How do I fit into the greater community?

What relationships can help me to do something about this issue?

What is God already doing in the community regarding this issue?

Questions regarding Problem Identification:

How can I be a blessing to my community?

What is needed in this community regarding this issue?

What is God saying that I should do about this problem?

What are people expressing as concerns?

What is being overlooked?

Who is "falling through the cracks?"

Who should I be listening to regarding this problem?

What are they saying?

Questions regarding Solution Implementation:

How do we solve the problem?

What is in the way?

Who can help to solve the problem?

How have others addressed the problem?

What team is needed?

How will a potential solution affect others?

Whose council would be helpful?

How is the problem related to spiritual matters or the Bible?

What steps would get us closer to a solution?

Questions regarding Mentor Relationship:

Who needs to know about ___?

What do I need to know concerning ___?

Who knows what I need to know?

What does the Bible say about ___?

What other books/authors can I learn from on this topic?

Who shares an interest in this topic and could potentially be someone to mentor?

Bibliography

Adair, John Eric. *How to Grow Leaders: The Seven Key Principles of Effective Leadership Development.* London Page, 2005.

Allen, Diogenes. *Spiritual Theology: The Theology of Yesterday for Spiritual Help Today.* NY: Cowley Publications, 1997.

Appiah, Albert. "Leadership Development in the Church: Renewal Christian Center, Maryland." Diss. Assemblies of God Theological Seminary, 2007.

Avolio, Bruce J., and Bernard M. Bass. *Developing Potential across a Full Range of Leadership: Cases on Transactional and Transformational Leadership.* Mahwah: 2002.

Barna, George. "Nothing is More Important than Leadership." *Leaders on Leadership.* Ed. George Barna. Ventura: Regal, 1997. 17-30. Print.

Bartz, James P. "Leadership from the Inside Out." *Anglican Theological Review* 91.1 (2009): 81-92. *ATLA Religion Database with ATLA Serials.* Web. 20 Feb. 2013.

Baveja, Alok, and Gayle Porter. "Creating an Environment for Personal Growth." *Advances in Interdisciplinary Studies of Work Teams* 3 (1996): 127-43.

Beh, Soo Yeong. "Leadership Development in the Local Church." Diss. Asbury Theological Seminary, 2012.

Bell, Skip. "Learning, Changing, and Doing: A Model for Transformational Leadership Development in Religious and Non-Profit Organizations." *Journal of Religious Leadership* 9.1 (2010): 93-111. *ATLA Religion Database with ATLA Serials.* Web. 20 Feb. 2013.

Blackaby, Henry T., and Richard Blackaby. *Spiritual Leadership: Moving People on to God's Agenda.* Nashville: Broadman, 2001.

Bradberry, Travis, and Jean Greaves. *Emotional Intelligence 2.0.* San Diego: TalentSmart, 2009.

Burke, Lisa A., and Holly M. Hutchins. "A Study of Best Practices in Training Transfer and Proposed Model of Transfer." *Human Resource Development Quarterly* 19:2 (2008): 107-125.

Callahan, Kennon L. *Effective Church Leadership: Building on the Twelve Keys*. San Francisco: Harper & Row, 1990.

Campbell, Regi, and Richard Chancy. *Mentor Like Jesus*. Nashville: Broadman, 2009. Print.

Cenac, Julianne. "Leader Emergence and the Phenomenological Work of the Holy Spirit in Acts 2." *Journal of Biblical Perspectives in Leadership* 3.1 (2010): 123-35. *Regent.edu*. Web. 13 March 2013.

Chand, Samuel R. *Cracking Your Church's Culture Code: Seven Keys to Unleashing Vision and Inspiration*. San Francisco: Jossey-Bass, 2011.

Clinton, James Robert. "Leadership Development Theory: Comparative Studies among High Level Christian Leaders." Diss. Fuller Theological Seminary, 1989.

---. *Mentoring: Developing Leaders through Empowering Relationships*. *Bobbyclinton.com*. Barnabas Publishers, 1997. Web. 31 Jan. 2013.

Clinton, Richard W. *Selecting & Developing Emerging Leaders*. Altadena: Barnabas, 1996.

Collins, James C. *Good to Great: Why Some Companies Make the Leap… and Others Don't*. New York: Harper, 2001.

Creps, Earl. *Off-Road Disciplines: Spiritual Adventures of Missional Leaders*. San Francisco: Jossey-Bass, 2006.

---. *Reverse Mentoring: How Young Leaders Can Transform the Church and Why We Should Let Them*. San Francisco: Jossey-Bass, 2008.

Crouch, Andy. *Culture Making: Recovering Our Creative Calling*. Downers Grove: InterVarsity, 2008.

Damazio, Frank. *The Strategic Church: A Life-Changing Church in an Ever-Changing Culture.* Ventura: Regal, 2012.

DePree, Max. *Leadership Is an Art.* New York: Doubleday, 1989.

Dodd, Brian J. *Empowered Church Leadership: Ministry in the Spirit According to Paul.* Downers Grove: InterVarsity, 2003.

Dunnam, Maxie and Kimberly Dunnam Reisman. *The Workbook on the Seven Deadly Sins.* Nashville: Upper Room Books, 1997.

Elliston, Edgar J. *Home Grown Leaders.* Pasadena: Carey Library, 1992.

Ford, Leighton. *Transforming Leadership: Jesus' Way of Creating Vision, Shaping Values & Empowering Change.* Downers Grove: InterVarsity, 1991.

Forman, Rowland, Jeff Jones, and Bruce Miller. *The Leadership Baton: An Intentional Strategy for Developing Leaders in Your Church.* Grand Rapids: Zondervan, 2004.

Geiger, Eric, Michael Kelley, and Philip Nation. *Transformational Discipleship: How People Really Grow.* Nashville: Broadman, 2012.

Gibbs, Eddie. *LeadershipNext: Changing Leaders in a Changing Culture.* Downers Grove: InterVarsity, 2005.

Hughes, Richard L., Robert C. Ginnett, and Gordon J. Curphy. *Leadership: Enhancing the Lessons of Experience.* 6th ed. Boston: McGrawIrwin, 2009.

Huizing, Russell L. "Leaders from Disciples: The Church's Contribution to Leadership Development." *Evangelical Review of Theology* 35.4 (2011): 333-44. *ATLA Religion Database with ATLA Serials.* Web. 20 Feb. 2013.

Hybels, Bill. *Courageous Leadership.* Grand Rapids: Zondervan, 2002.

Krallmann, Günter. *Mentoring for Mission: A Handbook on Leadership Principles Exemplified by Jesus Christ*. 2nd ed. Waynesburo: Gabriel, 2002.

Lance, Laura K. Message to the Author, 28 Mar. 2013. E-Mail.

Lewis, Robert, Wayne Cordeiro, and Warren Bird. *Culture Shift: Transforming Your Church from the Inside Out*. San Francisco: Jossey-Bass, 2005.

Long, Jimmy. *The Leadership Jump: Building Partnerships between Existing and Emerging Christian Leaders*. Downers Grove: InterVarsity, 2009.

Mallory, Sue. *The Equipping Church: Serving Together to Transform Lives*. Grand Rapids: Zondervan, 2001.

Malphurs, Aubrey. *Being Leaders: The Nature of Authentic Christian Leadership*. Grand Rapids: Baker, 2003.

Malphurs, Aubrey, and Will Mancini. *Building Leaders: Blueprints for Developing Leadership at Every Level of Your Church*. Grand Rapids: Baker, 2004.

Manning, Brennan. *Abba's Child: The Cry of the Heart for Intimate Belonging*. Expanded ed. Colorado Springs: NavPress, 2002.

Maxwell, John C. *Developing the Leaders around You*. Nashville: Nelson, 1995.

McNeal, Reggie. *Practicing Greatness: 7 Disciplines of Extraordinary Spiritual Leaders*. San Francisco: Jossey-Bass, 2006.

---. *A Work of Heart: Understanding How God Shapes Spiritual Leaders*. San Francisco: Jossey-Bass, 2000.

Miller, Calvin. *Into the Depths of God*. Minneapolis: Bethany House, 2000.

Minatrea, Milfred. *Shaped by God's Heart: The Passion and Practices of Missional Churches*. San Francisco: Jossey-Bass, 2004.

Moving with God Now: Mid-Atlantic District. "Mid-Atlantic District Annual Assembly Journal." *Manaz.org*. The Church of the Nazarene, 2012. Web. 13 Jan. 2013.

Muto, Susan and Adrian van Kaam. *Growing through the Stress of Ministry*. Totowa, NJ: Catholic Book Publishing Corp., 2005.

Nauta, Rein. "People Make the Place: Religious Leadership and the Identity of the Local Congregation." *Pastoral Psychology* 56.1 (2007): 45-52. *ATLA Religion Database with ATLA Serials*. Web. 20 Feb. 2013.

Nazarene Congregational Data Search. *Nazarene.org*. The Church of the Nazarene, 2013. Web. 22 April 2013.

Nees, Tom. "Where are the Leaders?" Online posting. *LeadingtoServe.com*. Leading to Serve, 2010. Web. 30 Sept. 2013.

Nouwen, Henri J. *A Spirituality of Waiting: Being Alert to God's Presence in Our Lives,* in *Weavings*, Nashville: The Upper Room, volume 11, number 1, Jan./Feb. 1987.

O'Day, Gail. "John." *The New Interpreter's Bible vol. IX*. Nashville: Abingdon Press, 1995.

Oden, Thomas C. *Life in the Spirit*. San Francisco: HarperSanFrancisco, 1992.

_____. *The Word of Life*. San Francisco: Harper & Row, 1989.

Ortberg, John. *God is Closer Than You Think*. Grand Rapids: Zondervan, 2005.

Peterson, Eugene. *The Pastor: A Memoir*. New York: HarperOne, 2011.

Petrie, Nick. *Future Trends in Leadership Development*. *Ccl.org*. Center for Creative Leadership, 2011. Web. 12 Feb. 2013.

Pue, Carson. *Mentoring Leaders: Wisdom for Developing Character, Calling, and Competency*. Grand Rapids: Baker, 2005.

Purves, Andrew. *Reconstructing Pastoral Theology: A Christological Foundation*. Louisville: Westminster-Knox, 2004.

Raelin, Joseph A. *Creating Leaderful Organizations: How to Bring Out Leadership in Everyone*. San Francisco: Berrett-Koehler, 2003.

Sciarra, Mike. "Leadership Development in the Local Church." Video. *Vimeo.com*. Vimeo, 2012. Web. 8 Feb. 2013.

Seamands, Stephen A. *Ministry in the Image of God: The Trinitarian Shape of Christian Service*. Downers Grove: InterVarsity, 2005.

Springle, Pat. *Developing Leaders in a Postmodern World: Current Principles and Practices in Selecting and Equipping Leaders. Leadnet.org*. Leadership Network, 2009. Web. 12 Feb. 2013.

Stott, John R. W. *Basic Christian Leadership: Biblical Models of Church, Gospel, and Ministry*. Downers Grove: InterVarsity, 2002.

Thumma, Scott, and Warren Bird. *The Other 80 Percent: Turning Your Church's Spectators into Active Participants*. San Francisco: Jossey-Bass, 2011.

VanderLugt, Dan, and Kurt DeHaan. *Who Qualifies to Be a Church Leader?* Discoveryseries.org. RBC Ministries, 2002. Web. 20 Feb. 2013.

VanderStoep, Scott W., and Deirdre D. Johnston. *Research Methods for Everyday Life: Blending Qualitative and Quantitative Approaches*. San Francisco: Jossey-Bass, 2009.

Von Rad, Gerhard. *Genesis: A Commentary*. 2nd ed., rev ed. London: SCM, 1963.

Wesley, John. *A Plain Account of Christian Perfection*. Kansas City, MO: Beacon Hill Press of Kansas City, 1966.

West, Russell W. *The What of Leadership Development: Toward an Emergence Culture*. Lexington: The Emergence Group, 2009. Print. Organizational Development White Paper Ser.

Wilkes, C. Gene. *Jesus on Leadership*. Wheaton: Tyndale, 1998.

Willard, Dallas. *Renovation of the Heart: Putting on the Character of Christ*. Colorado Springs: Nav Press, 2002.

Woodward, J. R. *Creating a Missional Culture: Equipping the Church for the Sake of the World*. Downers Grove: Praxis-InterVarsity, 2012.

Yaconelli, Michael. *Messy Spirituality: God's Annoying Love for Imperfect People*. Grand Rapids: Zondervan, 2002.

www.ingramcontent.com/pod-product-compliance
Lightning Source LLC
Chambersburg PA
CBHW081749100526
44592CB00015B/2349